A Pearl of Hope

A True Story By Tatyana Alekseyevna

Edited by Amy Bell

www.xulonpress.com

For God, my faithful Father who delivered me from the darkest depths of despair, mended my broken heart and filled my soul with joy, love and hope.

Table of Contents

Prologue ix

Chapter 1: The Accident 11

Chapter 2: A Sense of Dread 22

Chapter 3: Peace and Quiet 31

Chapter 4: Missing Mommy 44

Chapter 5: The Unthinkable 57

Chapter 6: Hospital 75

Chapter 7: The Trip 95

Chapter 8: Papa's News 113

Chapter 9: Not Alone 126

Chapter 10: A New Life 148

Epilogue 166

Prologue

𝒮

My past holds a hidden tragedy. The people I encounter every day would never imagine that my childhood was cut short by turmoil and heartache. I sometimes have a hard time believing it myself. But it is true. There is a horrible secret lurking in the darkest depths of my soul—and I must bring it to light.

I am happily married to an incredible man, and we have two wonderful sons who are truly gifts from God. I am a practicing dental hygienist, and I enjoy chatting with my patients, asking about their families and learning about their lives. Of course, I would never dare reveal my terrible past to them. When people meet me, they see a joyful, spiritual woman who loves life and lives each day to the fullest. But there is so much more to my story.

As I write this, I am thirty years old. I never thought I would share my story this early in life…but I know it is time.

It is time to dig deep into my past, unearth my tragic secret and reveal it to the world. It is time to offer hope to others who have lived through horrific tragedies that haunt their hearts and eat away at their souls; time to reach out to men and women who have lost hope and show them that with God, anything is possible. I am living proof of this undeniable fact.

When I look back on my life, I am absolutely astounded. I now realize that I am a walking miracle—in every sense of the word.

My story begins when I was a little girl growing up in Ukraine.

Chapter 1

The Accident

The day of my mother's accident—the day that would forever change our lives—the apricot sun shone brightly overhead in a cloudless sky. It was a balmy, sun-drenched afternoon, and my twin sister Natasha and I were walking home from school, giggling and chatting about the boys in our class. My sister and I took our time. We were in no rush to get home and face our chores on such a glorious day.

We skipped hand-in-hand, stopping to pluck dandelions from the grass and tuck them behind our ears. We sat by the side of the road, turning our faces up to the brilliant topaz sky, bathing in the warmth of the sun. It was a divine day, and everything was good and right with the world.

Back at home, my mother and grandmother were washing dishes side by side. Our grandmother, who we called Babushka, was visiting from Kharkov to help out around the house and spend some quality time with us. As they scrubbed dirty pots and pans, Babushka told my mother funny stories about her childhood. Their girlish laughter drifted out of the open windows and into the backyard.

Out back, my older brother Sasha sat eating a handful of blackberries in the shade of our Macintosh apple tree. The towering tree, which stood right next to our outdoor bathroom, had been mostly dead for as long as I could remember. As busy as my parents were, I guess they hadn't found the time to chop it down. So there it stood, brown and withered, wasting away in our backyard.

Feeling particularly playful on this sunny day, Sasha was suddenly overcome with a burst of childish energy. He decided to climb the old tree. He shimmied up the trunk until he found a hidden, shady seat about fifteen feet above the ground. Perched atop a dried out branch, he could see the entire backyard.

Just then, our mother strolled out of the house and into the backyard. "Look at me, Mommy!" Sasha shouted down to her. Mother stopped by the back door and turned her gaze to the top of the tree, shielding her emerald eyes with a delicate hand. The sunlight glinted off her chocolate hair as she smiled up at Sasha. "You be careful up there!" she said. She started walking toward the outdoor bathroom. "Aren't I strong?" Sasha yelled down, beaming. "I climbed all the way up here all by my..."

Sasha was interrupted by a deafening, CRACK...POP! It rang out like a gunshot. His heart plunged into his stomach as he realized the branch beneath him was breaking. He quickly grabbed onto the limb above him and wrapped his legs around the thick tree trunk. His chest pounding, Sasha watched the large branch plummet toward the ground, where Mother was walking beneath the tree.

"MOMMY, NO!" he shrieked. But it was too late. The branch crashed directly on my mother's head with a loud thump. "Owww!" she bellowed, slumping to the ground. Sasha quickly scaled down the tree and crouched next to our mother's limp body.

****

I was one of seven children, but only six of us were my mother's biological children. Sasha, my oldest brother, came from my father's first marriage.

At the age of eighteen my father married a young woman named Vera. Soon after their wedding, they had a baby boy and named him Sasha. When Sasha turned two, his mother developed a terrible health condition that left her paralyzed. As the days and weeks passed, Vera grew sicker and weaker, and Papa watched helplessly as she wilted into a fragile shell. One frigid winter night, Papa found Vera shrouded in mounds of wool blankets on her bed—her bony body cold and lifeless. Papa was devastated. A heart-broken widower with a motherless toddler, my father spent the following weeks stumbling numbly through his days ... until he caught a glimpse of my mother.

It was only one year after Vera's death when Papa first laid eyes on her. Mother was a beautiful woman, slender with radiant green eyes and cascading chocolate hair. She was instantly drawn to Papa's captivating sapphire eyes, as blue as the crisp autumn sky. He was thin with chestnut hair and a voice as smooth as milk. She could detect the loneliness and heartache behind his feeble smile, and she wanted more than anything to comfort him.

Papa and Mommy were married in 1979. Only weeks after their wedding, my mother became pregnant with not one, but two babies. On November 3, 1979, my twin sister Natasha and I were born.

They named me after my mother's younger sister, who had a birth mark on her right cheek. When my mother held me for the first time, she noticed the same cinnamon-colored smudge on my tiny face. "We'll name this one Tatyana," Mommy announced, stroking my petal-soft cheek with her finger.

Natasha and I were such identical babies that even our parents had a hard time telling us apart. But when Mommy and Papa spotted the birth mark, they knew it was me, baby Tatyana.

Throughout my mother's pregnancy, Aunt Tatyana had been in the Kharkov hospital receiving treatment for severe asthma complications. A few days after Natasha and I were born, there was a knock at my parents' front door. My mother swung open the door to find Tatyana standing there, her fragile body shivering in the bitter cold. She refused to let her illness keep her from us.

"What are you doing here?" my mother scolded as she pulled Aunt Tatyana in the house. Mommy was worried, but she was secretly thrilled to see her little sister.

"I came to see the babies," Tatyana replied with a smiling, ashen face.

Aunt Tatyana had sneaked out of the hospital, quietly slipping out a back door into the brutally cold night. She had taken a train all the way from downtown Kharkov. My mother was upset with Tatyana for risking her health, but she understood her sister's intentions. Aunt Tatyana had a huge heart, and there was no stopping her when she set her mind to something.

"I cannot believe you came all this way…and in your condition!" My mother embraced her delicate sister and kissed her gently on the pale cheek. "Come now," she said, as she walked down the hallway. "You need to drink some hot tea."

"Where are they, where are the babies?" Tatyana kept asking, as she shuffled after my mother into the kitchen. "I can't wait to see them."

"They are sleeping now, but they'll probably wake soon," mother said. She stood on her tiptoes and pulled two flowered tea cups from the cupboard. "Now, sit down, and I'll make some tea."

When Natasha and I finally awoke, Aunt Tatyana took turns holding us. Ecstatic to finally meet her twin nieces, she could barely contain her excitement. She giggled and clapped and cooed at us.

"Now, don't get too excited, Tatyana," mother warned her little sister. "You know that brings on your asthma attacks."

Tatyana just waved away my mother's comments with a smile. She sang sweet lullabies to our sleepy faces and covered our downy heads with kisses.

After her brief evening with us, Aunt Tatyana returned to the hospital. She knitted little socks for Natasha and me in her hospital bed. She finished my socks, but she never completed Natasha's. Aunt Tatyana passed away when we were just a few weeks old. She was only sixteen.

Before she died, Tatyana saw angels. As the family surrounded her death bed, Tatyana pointed to the hospital ceiling and rasped, "Don't you see those divine creatures flying overhead?" Mother said my aunt was in such peace before she departed this earth. Those lovely angels must have comforted Aunt Tatyana before they embraced her soul and flew it straight to Heaven.

"You know," my mother once told me, "Tatyana was the sweetest girl in my family."

I thought it was an incredible honor to carry on her name.

Over the next ten years, my parents had four more babies. By 1989, the year of my family's tragedy, our house was swarming with seven children. Sasha was thirteen, and Natasha and I were ten. Our younger brother Misha was eight, and little sisters Vera and Alonna were six and four. Our youngest sister, baby Julia, was only nine months old.

Because my father worked the night shift at a factory and slept during the day, my mother handled everything around the house. At the young age of twenty-nine, she was taking care of seven children and juggling all the household chores. It was a demanding and thankless job.

Mother had a giving heart and was always friendly and kind to others. Whenever we had guests, she would only offer them the best that we had—even if that wasn't much. But Mommy was not always a joyful person. She had a lot on her hands, and she was overwhelmed and exhausted most of the time.

After baby Julia was born, Sasha often overheard Mommy sobbing softly in the kitchen. The stress of raising seven children must have been too much to bear at times, and her emotions would come bubbling out of her. I realize now that my mother may have suffered from postpartum depression. But like every other Ukrainian mother with a house full of children, she kept pressing on, day after day, week after week.

I was definitely the naughtiest child, and I often pushed my mother over the edge with my antics.

"Tatyana, you never listen!" she would hiss. "You are going to send me to an early grave."

I always felt so guilty when she uttered those words. Almost every night, I would cry myself to sleep and beg God to forgive me for my bad behavior.

One time, my parents invited some friends over for a meal. My mother was planning to serve sosiski, which are like gourmet hot dogs of smoked pork with clear casing. She had purchased one for each guest. That afternoon, as mother scurried around cleaning and preparing for our visitors, I was overcome with hunger. I crept into the kitchen, quietly opened the refrigerator door and took a peek at the sosiski. They looked and smelled absolutely scrumptious, and my mouth watered at the sight of them. Before I knew it, I had gobbled one up. I knew what I was doing was wrong, but I hoped for the best. "Maybe she won't notice," I thought as I wandered back to my bedroom with a full stomach.

A few minutes later, my mother screeched furiously from the kitchen, "Who ate the sosiska?" No one answered.

She angrily gathered all the children and lined us up in front of the kitchen table. She went down the row of our concerned little faces, asking us one by one, "Did you eat the sosiska?"

"No, Mommy," answered Natasha. "You told us *not* to eat them."

"Vera?"

"Nuh-uh," Vera shook her head with a pout. "I promise... I didn't."

She continued down the line until, finally, it was my turn.

"Tatyana, did you eat the sosiska?"

"No, not me," I stammered, as my cheeks flushed crimson. Of course, my mother always knew when I was telling a lie because my face turned bright red.

Without hesitation, she grabbed the rod from the closet and started spanking me. I cried for mercy, but there was none to be had.

Between my sobs and pleas, an idea popped into my head. My mother had once told me that when I was very little, if someone tickled me too hard, I would faint. We weren't sure why it happened, but Mommy always warned people about my strange condition. It had been years since I'd fainted...but that's exactly what I decided to do. In the middle of the spanking, I went limp and slumped to the floor.

My mother immediately stopped spanking me and knelt down next to my head.

"Tatyana!" she shrieked frantically. "Tatyana, are you okay?" I could hear the terror in her trembling voice. She scooped me up, carried me to her bedroom and laid me on the bed.

As I sprawled lifelessly on my mother's bed, all of my brothers and sisters surrounded my wilted body, peering down at me with worried little faces. I forced myself to remain absolutely motionless—I feared that if I made even the slightest movement, Mommy would know I was faking. Soon, my brothers and sisters began to pray in quiet, quivering voices. My mother patted my head and gently shook my body, crying my name over and over, "Tatyana? Tatyana, oh please!"

I felt terrible, but I knew I had to keep up the sham—or else my punishment would be a million times worse. After a few more minutes, I pretended to regain consciousness, slowly opening my blue eyes. My mother embraced me, stroking my hair as she rocked me back and forth in her arms. "Oh, Tatyana, I'm so sorry," she whispered. "I never meant to hurt you."

That night, I silently prayed for forgiveness. "Please God, forgive me for lying to Mommy," I whispered into my pillow. "Please, please forgive me." I drifted off into a black, dreamless sleep with that constant prayer on my lips.

To this day, I don't know if my mother ever realized I was faking. And I still feel guilty for my naughty little fainting act.

Chapter 2

A Sense of Dread

"Oh God, it HURTS! *Ohhh*," Mommy moaned as she trembled in the grass at the bottom of the withered apple tree. She held her hands to her head, tossing and turning on the ground, her fragile body wracked with sobs.

"Mommy, I'm so sorry," Sasha whispered as he knelt next to her, tears streaming down his cheeks. "Oh mother, please forgive me. Please, I'm so, so sorry. I didn't mean to hurt you." One of Sasha's salty tears splashed onto Mother's quivering hand.

After a few minutes, her whimpering died off. She suddenly sat up, her hands still on her head. "It's okay, Sasha," she said in a shaky voice. "I'll be okay."

Sasha held onto mother's feeble arms and helped her to her feet. For what seemed like an eternity, Mommy stood completely still with a dazed, distant look behind her glassy eyes. "Okay," she finally broke the silence. "Okay, time to get back to work."

With one hand still resting on top of her head, Mother stumbled toward the barn. Unsure what to do, Sasha rushed inside and found Babushka drying dishes in the kitchen.

"B-b-babushka," he stammered between sobs. "Something terrible has happened to Mommy."

Babushka tossed the dishrag to the floor. "Where is she?" she said as she raced out the back door.

"In the barn!" Sasha called after her.

Babushka found our mother preparing food for the livestock in the barn, her back turned to the door. "What happened?" Babushka asked, gently touching her daughter on the shoulder. As my mother turned around, Babushka was shocked to see her daughter's face white as chalk, her emerald eyes dulled to a lifeless gray.

"Oh my," Babushka cried. "You're white as a ghost. Are you sick?"

My mother didn't respond right away. But after a few moments of silent confusion, she burst into tears and fell into Babushka's arms. She explained what had happened beneath the tree, and then pulled away to show Babushka her wound.

Babushka gasped at the sight of it. In the center of Mommy's head, where the branch had smashed into her crown, there was a small concavity—like a deeply dented apple.

An overwhelming sense of dread swept over Babushka, and she felt her pulse quicken with anxiety. She hugged my mother tightly, holding onto her damaged daughter for dear life.

****

We lived in a modest, three-bedroom house in a small rural town called Lubotin. I shared a room with all of my brothers and sisters—except for baby Julia, who slept in a crib in Mommy and Papa's room.

Our house always felt cramped, but we made the most of what we had, which wasn't much. We did not have a toilet in the house, so we had to use an outdoor bathroom.

We had a small kitchen with a coal-burning stove, a refrigerator, a table and a little sink. Because there was no water line leading into the house, we took turns going outside to pump water for the sink.

My siblings and I would wash up a little every day in the kitchen, but we got to take a real bath in my parents' stainless steel bathtub once a week. My mother filled the tub with warm water, and everyone took turns bathing in it. We all looked forward to this weekly treat.

The guest bedroom was the nicest room in our house. Not only was it decorated with the finest furniture we owned, but Mother always kept the room immaculate in case family members or friends decided to visit. We children were never allowed to enter this perfectly preserved room.

"Stay out of there!" Mommy would shout every time one of us walked within a stone's throw of the forbidden guest room. We always wondered if she was hiding something in there, some shadowy secret sealed up tightly behind the heavy wooden door.

So we tried to steer clear of the guest bedroom—and our moody Mother—by spending most of our time outside. Our little brick house overlooked a tidy front yard bursting with apple trees, cherry trees and an array of colorful flowers. In the fenced backyard, behind the detached garage where Papa stored his car and motorcycle, we kept a small garden filled with raspberry and blackberry bushes. Our neighbors had a plum tree, and a few of the branches grew over the fence into our yard. My brothers and sisters and I would climb the fence to pick the purple gems, and we'd sit in the grass savoring the succulent fruit, sticky juice streaming down our arms.

We had a big German shepherd named Reks. He lived outside, so he was always a little smelly and matted—but we loved to play with him, chasing him through the yard and throwing sticks for him to fetch. Reks knew us as his owners, but he would have torn a stranger apart. Papa always warned us to be careful with him. "*Never* trust a dog," he would say in his stern voice.

My siblings and I played outside all the time, no matter what the season. In the winter, we took turns skiing and pulling each other on sleds through nearby fields. In the spring and summer, we would dig in the dirt, shaping the damp soil into stars and hearts and setting them out to dry in the sun. In the fall, Natasha and I threw pretend tea parties, serving brilliantly colored "salads" made from grass and autumn leaves.

From our house, it took fifteen minutes to walk to the nearest train stop, which was next to the grocery store. Although we could not see the railroad tracks from our house, we could certainly hear them. I remember falling asleep to the screeching and whistling of trains as they chugged down the dark tracks.

Lubotin was a calm, quiet little city. Everyone knew each other, and all the neighborhood children played together. But unlike our neighbors, we were a Christian family.

We went to a large, conservative church in the city of Kharkov. The men and women sat on opposite sides of the aisle, and we girls had to cover our heads with little silk scarves. My siblings and I attended the children's ministry. We had to memorize verses from the Bible, and on holidays we would recite them before the church congregation.

Although my parents were always busy taking care of us and working, they tried to stay active in the church. Mommy sang in the choir, and Papa sometimes preached. He had been preaching since he was just sixteen years old, when he would visit villages to teach the gospel. When he was young, Papa never turned down an opportunity to preach.

It came as no surprise to me that our church members enjoyed my father's preaching. He was a handsome, charming man. Although he was slim when he first married my mother, he filled out nicely as he grew older. People were drawn to his kind eyes and calming voice. Papa was always an optimist who loved life, and he saw each day as a gift.

My parents were extremely hard workers, but it was a challenge to keep us all fed and clothed. Papa toiled away as a plumber in a factory night after night, but the nine of us still struggled to live off his meager earnings.

Still, every now and then, Papa would surprise us with a special treat.

"Who wants to go to the zoo?" Papa shouted one pay day as he burst through the front door.

He was greeted by a chorus of excited squeals. "I do, I do!" Natasha and I sang as Vera, Alonna and Misha giggled with delight.

We walked to the railroad station and took a half-hour train ride to the bustling city. We were always excited about visiting Kharkov. All the roads were paved, and the city was filled with beautiful monuments, towering buildings, an airport and even an underground subway. It was an exhilarating place to visit, especially for small-town children like us. When we arrived at the Kharkov Zoo, we spent the afternoon munching on fluffy pink cotton candy and admiring the elephants, bears and snakes.

However, trips to the zoo were rare. Most of the time, we were lucky just to have enough food to go around.

****

When Natasha and I finally made it home from school the day of my mother's accident, we were surprised to find Babushka cooking dinner. Mommy always cooked for us, even when Babushka was visiting.

"Girls, your mother is not well," Babushka said in a solemn voice. "She's resting in her bedroom now, so please do not disturb her. Now run along and help Sasha clean the barn."

Natasha and I looked at each other wide-eyed, but we obeyed our grandmother.

When we found Sasha sulking in the barn, he told us what had happened. Natasha burst into tears, but I was too afraid to cry. The thought of losing our mother terrified me into silence. I felt as if our family was precariously perched on some sort of fateful tightrope. If I made any sudden moves or spoke too loudly, we might lose our balance and plunge into the darkest depths of disaster.

As I delicately swept out the barn alongside Natasha, I breathed a hushed prayer, begging the Lord to spare our mother. "Please Lord, we can't survive without Mommy," I pleaded. "Please don't take her away from us."

Early the next morning, Papa returned home after working the night shift at the factory. My mother shuffled down the hall to meet him at the front door, and Papa bellowed, "Good morning, dear!" as he shook off his coat. But as soon as he lifted his cold-flushed face and caught a glimpse of mother, his smile melted and he fell silent.

Mother's head was wrapped tightly with a crisp, white cloth, and her face had taken on a yellow hue. "Dear Lord," my father exclaimed. "Are you sick? What on earth happened?"

As she told Papa about the accident, I saw terror flash behind his sky blue eyes. But when he realized Natasha and I were peeking out of the kitchen and peering down the hallway, he quickly masked his troubled face with a grin. "Why don't we get you back to bed?" Papa said, trying to sound calm. But he was not calm at all...I could tell by his furrowed brow that he was sick with worry.

Chapter 3

Peace and Quiet

Before the accident, Mommy had a long list of tasks to accomplish each day, so she was always busy. She took time to hug us and tell us she loved us, but we didn't get to spend a lot of quality time with her.

Nevertheless, I loved my mother dearly. I constantly told her so. I always longed to touch her arm or bury my face in her chocolate tresses and breathe in her syrupy scent. She smelled sweeter than the delicious trubochki we made with her one glorious day.

I still remember every detail of that special morning. The sugary aroma of the baking trubochki mingled with the soft music drifting from the radio, filling the house with peaceful joy. All of the children waited patiently as the sweet treat baked in the pizzelle maker.

When the pastries were ready, we chattered with excitement. We surrounded Mommy in the kitchen, helping her roll the trubochki and stuff creamy filling into the cone-shaped delicacies.

"Now be very careful," Mommy calmly instructed. "The cookies are very crunchy and fragile, so they can easily break."

As Misha lifted a rolled cookie to his mouth, Mommy scolded, "No, no, Misha. Don't eat them before you put the filling inside!"

Misha looked up at her with round, innocent eyes and answered, "But Mommy...it smells so *good!*" We all burst into a chorus of giggles—even Mommy chuckled along with us.

A sense of comfort spread throughout my soul. I felt so complete and safe. It was the last time I can remember feeling that way as a child.

****

My siblings and I adored Mommy, and we always wanted to please her with kind gestures. One year, a few days before my mother's birthday, all of the children came together for a meeting.

"How much do you have, Tatyana?" Sasha asked.

I shook my change purse, and three shiny coins fell to the floor with a clang. "That's it," I frowned.

"Okay...what about the rest of you?" Sasha said.

One by one, each child presented their meager savings. We scraped together every coin, but it only added up to a couple of rubles. We decided to buy mother some decorative hair pins. It was all we could afford. Of course, she was delighted with our gift, no matter how small and insignificant it seemed to us. "How sweet, my children," she said proudly as she pinned a wavy strand of hair away from her face. "Thank you!"

My family didn't have much, but we did what we had to do to survive. When we weren't in school, especially in the summers, Natasha and I looked after the little ones while Sasha helped mother with household chores. Sasha was such a great helper to our family. He knew how to do everything.

He would walk to the grocery store to buy butter, fish, sugar and bread, and he helped my mother work in the barn and feed the livestock. Because we were such a large family, we owned a cow, pigs and chickens. Owning livestock wasn't a luxury—it was a means of survival. The animals helped us put food on our table.

A few of our neighbors owned goats, but we were the only family with a cow and pigs. My brother Sasha had to walk the cow down paved roads to the grazing fields, and he often received strange looks from the neighbors. I was embarrassed for him, and I know he was humiliated—but Sasha never complained.

Sometimes Natasha and I would join Sasha on his cow walk of shame. Once we reached the field, we would build a fire together. As the cow grazed, the three of us would sit by the small blaze, telling stories and giggling in the warm, orange glow.

As I was growing up, I never felt like Sasha was a half-brother. Although he had a different mother, I always knew him as my true brother.

I adored all of my brothers and sisters. Since we didn't have much, we always had to find creative ways to entertain ourselves—and we spent countless hours playing together. We didn't have a lot of toys, but there were a few dolls for the girls and some cars for the boys. There was also a piano in our bedroom, so we took turns tapping out church songs.

We also spent a lot of time make-believing. We loved to play "Church" or pretend that someone was getting married.

"I get to be the bride this time!" Natasha exclaimed one afternoon.

"Okay," I giggled. "And Misha will be the groom. Vera and Alonna, you'll be the bridesmaids, and...I'll be the preacher!" I announced. "I'll go get the costumes," I yelled as I sprinted from our bedroom.

I skipped through our parents' room and the kitchen and down the hallway. I yanked open a small door and climbed the stairs to the attic. As I breezed past the homemade kielbasa (sausage) my mother had hung up to dry, I caught a glimpse of a bluebird flying by the tiny attic window. Hoping to get a closer look, I stood on my tiptoes and peeked through the glass. Reks was sitting in the yard panting, his long pink tongue curling from his mouth. "Silly dog," I muttered. I walked over to a large trunk, threw open the lid and scooped up a handful of old clothes. Suddenly, I felt a little frightened to be all alone in that dusty old attic, and a chill ran down my spine. I raced back down the stairs and into the hallway as quickly as my legs would carry me.

When I returned to our bedroom, I dumped the pile of clothes on the floor. After digging through my mother and father's musty old clothes, we each dressed up in ridiculously oversized suits and gowns.

We then launched into our disorderly wedding ceremony, which was constantly interrupted by peals of laughter and silly comments.

Finally, I announced, "And now, you may kiss the bride." Misha looked at me wide-eyed, scrunching up his freckled nose with disgust.

"Kiss the bride, Misha," Vera whispered. "It's not official till you kiss her!" she taunted. Alonna erupted into a fit of girly giggles.

Misha pushed his stiff lips as far away from his face as he could manage, and dryly pecked Natasha on the cheek. "EWWW!" he groaned as Alonna and Vera sniggered.

"You are now husband and wife!" I proclaimed as Misha linked arms with Natasha and bolted to the other side of the room.

"Hey, let's play Church now," I suggested.

"Okay," Natasha agreed. "But we need to find our Church preacher. Sasha!!!" she shouted, her tiny hands cupped over her mouth. "Where are you? We're ready for communion!" She scurried outside searching for our big brother, who always played the best preacher.

****

In the days following our mother's accident, my siblings and I were not quite as cheerful. Mommy stayed in bed all day, and she suffered from excruciating headaches.

"It feels like a hot teakettle is simmering on my head," she would whimper to my father, her ashen face twisted into a grimace of pain.

Papa told us not to disturb our mother. She just wanted to be alone in silence, so we were to stay out of her room unless she called for us.

But she never called. She barely even spoke. Natasha and I would quietly tiptoe past her room, trying to catch a glimpse of her colorless face. I thought maybe if I could see her, I would know whether or not she was going to survive.

A few days after the accident, my mother showed no signs of improvement. Papa took her to the hospital, where she told a doctor about her agonizing headaches. After our mother described her head injury and the type of pain she was experiencing, the doctor pulled Papa aside.

"She is no condition to go home," he said in a low voice as he jotted some notes on a clipboard. "She needs to stay here in the hospital where we can observe her."

"For how long?" Papa asked.

"As long as it takes her to recover," the doctor answered as he tucked the pen back into his coat pocket. "Could be a few days, a few weeks or even a few months...but we need to keep an eye on her."

Papa asked for a second opinion. After examining mother, the second doctor told my father it would be okay for her to rest and recover at home.

Still feeling uncertain, Papa met with a string of other doctors, and every one of them seemed to give a different diagnosis and a different recommendation. Bewildered by all the contradicting advice, my father did not know what to do. At that time in Ukraine, there were not many treatments available for head injuries, and many patients were misdiagnosed. One of the doctors told my father the only probable treatment for my mother was to send her to a mental hospital. Stunned by this suggestion, my father said a mental hospital was no place for his wife. He had another place in mind: America.

Some of Papa's friends had already moved to America, and they were very happy living there. In fact, before my mother's accident, Papa had applied for U.S. visas for our entire family—even though mother said she refused to move there. She had heard too many negative things about America, and she told Papa she would have no part of it. This had been an ongoing argument between the two of them.

But now Papa had an even greater motivation to move our family to the U.S.: He knew mother could get proper medical treatment there. So after weighing his options, Papa decided it would be best for our family if mother rested at home until our visas arrived in the mail. Then, he would quickly move us to America where she could get the best possible treatment for her head trauma. In the meantime, he would request a leave of absence from work so he could stay at home with us while Mommy recovered.

Before they left the hospital, one of the doctors prescribed some medication for Mommy's pain. Unfortunately, the local pharmacy did not have it in stock. The pharmacist said he would notify my father when the next shipment arrived. So, my mother went home with no treatment, no medication and no relief from her insufferable pain.

Because Mommy could not take care of us, Babushka decided to move in for a while to help out around the house until Papa could begin his leave of absence. She washed our clothes, cooked our meals and fed the animals. When Sasha wasn't at school, he helped Babushka as much as possible. All of the children had little jobs to do. We all pulled together to help out our sick mother.

"What you doin'?" Alonna asked Vera one day in the kitchen.

"I'm helping Babushka," Vera said as she dried the clean dishes. "We have to do our part because Mommy is sick."

"What wrong with Mommy? Why she no feel good?" Alonna asked with a pout.

"Her head hurts," Misha answered gloomily as he entered the room, a basket of clean laundry in his arms.

"*Oh, no!* Mommy has boo-boo on her head," Alonna whined. "I go kiss it!" she announced as she galloped towards our mother's bedroom door.

"No, wait Alonna!" I said, grabbing my little sister by her tiny arm. My heart broke for her. At just four years old, she was too young to understand what was happening.

I crouched down beside Alonna and said, "Papa told us not to bother Mommy. She's resting right now." Alonna's lower lip started to quiver.

"Hey, how about we go outside and pick some flowers, instead?" I said, trying to fake a happy voice. "I'll make you a grass salad!"

"Okay!" Alonna beamed. She grabbed me by the hand and pulled me to the front door.

Over the next few weeks, we had countless conversations like this with the younger siblings. They constantly peppered Papa and Babushka with questions about our mother.

"When will Mommy get better?"

"Why can't I go talk to Mommy?"

"What's wrong with Mommy's head?"

Papa responded to all of their questions as best as he could. But the truth was he didn't have the answers. No one did.

Although Mommy stayed in bed most of the time, she rarely slept. Whenever she would begin to doze off, the piercing headaches would drive away her dreams and violently rouse her from her sleep.

Her appetite had completely vanished, and she became furious when anyone tried to coax her to eat. One day, Babushka brought her a bowl of chicken broth with some crackers.

"You have got to get some food in that stomach," Babushka pleaded.

"Why are you making me eat?" Mother snapped. "How many times do I have to tell you, *I'm not hungry.*"

"You'll never regain your strength if you don't eat," Babushka replied softly. "Just take a couple of bites, and I'll leave you alone."

"Ugh, fine," Mother snarled as she shoveled a tiny cracker morsel in her mouth. "Anything to get some peace and quiet."

On the rare occasions when she had enough strength, Mother would try to help with the laundry. One day, Babushka found her throwing soiled shirts in a basket filled with freshly cleaned clothes.

"What are you doing?" Babushka asked. Mother stood up from the laundry basket and stared into the distance with a vacant look on her face.

"These are dirty, dear. They do not belong with the clean clothes," Babushka gently explained. Mother continued to stand there, one of my father's sweat-stained shirts dangling from her fingertips.

"I think it's time for you to head back to bed. I'll take care of this," Babushka said, attempting to hide her concern. My mother dropped the dirty shirt to the floor and ambled back to her bedroom without a word.

Our mother had also grown indifferent to baby Julia, who was only nine months old. She showed absolutely no affection or motherly passion for her youngest child. She no longer wanted to snuggle with Julia or feed her or sing silly songs to her as she had before the accident. When Babushka noticed this strange behavior, she realized Mommy's condition was much worse than we thought.

A few months after the accident, I was creeping past my parents' bedroom when I saw Papa packing some of Mother's clothes.

"What are you doing?" I asked, terrified that Mommy was leaving to stay in the hospital.

Startled, Papa looked up from the brown suitcase, a lavender dress dotted with tiny flowers in his hand. "Tatyana, your mother needs some peace and quiet," he said as he continued to fold clothes and carefully place them in mother's suitcase. "She's going to stay with Babushka in Kharkov for a while."

My heart plummeted into my stomach, and I felt anxiety wash over me. How could we live without our mother? What if she died while she was at Babushka's? What if I never had another chance to bury my face in her hair and breathe in her sweet scent?

Papa must have seen the concern on my face because he stopped folding clothes. He walked around the bed and knelt down in front of me, pulling me into his strong arms.

"It's going to be okay, Tatyana," he whispered in his soothing voice. "Mommy's going to stay with Babushka just until she can get her strength back, and then she'll come home. In the meantime, I will take care of you."

With a firm grip on my shoulders, Papa pulled away from me so he could see my face. "As long as we keep praying, God will take care of Mommy," he said, his blue eyes glistening. "God will take care of all of us."

Later that morning, I stood in the dusty driveway with Natasha, Misha, Alonna, Vera and Sasha, who was holding baby Julia. We all waved goodbye as Papa backed the car into the dirt road and headed toward the train station.

As they slowly pulled away, Papa honked the horn and Babushka waved energetically from the backseat. Through the passenger window, I caught a glimpse of Mother's pale, expressionless face. She did not smile or wave. She just stared in our direction as if she were looking straight through us—as if she could see something in the distance that we couldn't see.

Chapter 4

Missing Mommy

The next few months were extremely difficult for our family. Our house felt so cold and empty without Mommy's presence.

But Papa took care of us, and he tried his best to cheer us up. He loved all of his children dearly, and he showered us with affection while our mother was gone. He smothered us with kisses and tossed Vera, Alonna and Julia up in the air, until they exploded with irrepressible giggles.

One day after school, as Natasha and I walked into the front door, we were met by the delicious aroma of home-cooked food. My stomach immediately started to growl and my mouth watered. Natasha and I looked at each other with wild eyes, and she whispered, "Mommy's home!"

We raced down the hall to the kitchen to find Papa frying potatoes in a black skillet. He glanced over his shoulder with a grin and shouted, "Hi girls! How about some potatoes and sour cream?"

I was disappointed that our mother had not returned, but my stomach was still rumbling. Natasha and I sat at the table, and Papa placed a piping hot plate in front of each of us. We devoured the crunchy fried potatoes and frothy sour cream. They were the most delectable potatoes I had ever tasted.

A few nights later, I noticed that Alonna was unusually quiet at dinner. She picked at her food and then sat with her arms crossed with a miserable frown on her face. As soon as Papa started clearing the table, Alonna broke into a spine-tingling wail and fat tears poured from her squinted eyes.

"What's wrong, my little girl?" Papa asked, as he rushed over to Alonna's chair.

"I want Mommy!" Alonna sputtered through her tears. "When Mommy coming home, Papa? When she coming back?"

My father's face darkened with sadness, but he quickly masked it with a strained smile. "Mother will be coming home soon, I promise," he said, wiping the tears from Alonna's flushed cheeks. "But until then, I think we should take as many baths as we want—what do you think? Who's up for a nice warm, bath tonight?"

Alonna looked up at Papa with a confused scowl. But after a few moments, a grin spread across her tiny face. "Me," she whispered. "Me, me, Papa! I want a bath!"

Papa filled up the big stainless tub with balmy water, and we all took turns taking a bath. Once we were all clean, dressed in our pajamas and snuggled in our beds, Papa came into our bedroom to say goodnight. Baby Julia was already sound asleep in her crib in Papa's room.

"Papa, tell us a Bible story," Misha begged as he nestled under his big brown blanket. "Pleeeeeaaaase!"

"Okay, I can do that," Papa replied as he switched off our bedroom light. He told us about David and Goliath and Joseph the Dreamer, changing his voice as he spoke for the different characters. We all oohed and ahhed as we cuddled under our covers and listened intently to Papa's soothing voice. I felt warm and calm for the first time since mother's head injury.

"Good night, my dear children," Papa whispered as he left our room. "Sleep well."

As the door clicked shut behind Papa, all the cozy warmth suddenly rushed out of our bedroom and was replaced by a bone-chilling cold. Once again, I was over-come with fear of the unknown about what would happen to

Mommy. My chest burned with worry, and I shivered under my blanket. I listened to Natasha's breaths grow deeper as she fell asleep next to me.

I tossed and turned for what felt like hours, reciting prayers in my head: "Dear God, please let Mommy get better and come home to us. Please don't take her away from us." I repeated these pleas over and over until the words bled together into jumbled nonsense and I finally fell into a restless sleep.

****

While mother was away, the days seemed to stretch on endlessly. Sometimes the house was so painfully quiet, you could hear the clock ticking on the kitchen wall.

My brothers and sisters and I did not laugh and joke nearly as much as we had before. We were constantly worried about our mother, fearful that she would die from her excruciating pain. As we toiled away at our chores, we moped around with furrowed brows, weighed down with sadness, waiting on bated breath for Mommy to come home.

But for now, we had to make do without her. Papa's boss had not yet approved his leave of absence, so he was still working the night shift at the factory. When our father left for work in the evening, one of the nice ladies from our church would come over to keep an eye on us, cook dinner and tuck us into bed. One kind woman brought a ukulele and played music for us. Although the joyful tunes briefly lifted our spirits, it reminded me of how our mother used to sing and play her accordion. And before I knew it, my heart was aching with sorrow once again.

Natasha and I continued with our piano lessons, and that helped to pass the time. One day when we were practicing, we decided to make up a song for Mommy.

"Dearest mother, oh dearest mother...when will you come?" I sang in a shaky voice as Natasha and I slowly pecked at the piano keys.

"We miss you, our dearest mother. Please come home soon," Natasha crooned.

As the days turned into weeks and the weeks turned into months, we made up song after song. We looked forward to surprising mother with these homemade melodies when she got better and came back home.

I liked to imagine that when Mommy returned, she would be back to her old self, the way she was before the accident—or at least the way I liked to remember her. She would laugh and smile and toss her hair over her shoulder, her emerald eyes twinkling with life. She would carry baby Julia in her arms, cooing and singing hymns to her, stroking her chubby cheek. She would ask me how my day was at school and chuckle when I told her funny stories about my teacher and classmates. Her sweet scent would fill our home with warmth, and we would all feel a sense of security again. Although I liked to imagine my mother would return healthy and happy, I realized this fanciful dream would probably never come true. In reality, my siblings and I were all very worried. We were constantly haunted by the fear of what might happen to our mother, and it was draining the life out of us.

Back at Babushka's house in Kharkov, our mother was not doing well. She could not sleep. She simply lay in bed all day, staring at the cracked walls, as if she were lost deep in thought.

****

At church, Papa continued to hear stories about families immigrating to the United States, and he was anxious to move our family there. However, most Ukrainians had a negative opinion of the U.S. Back then, in 1989, Ukraine was still part of Soviet Union. It was a Communist country, and Ukrainian schools taught that there was no God. If you spoke about your religious faith in class, the other children would taunt and tease you. One time, I told my classmates that I was a Christian, and a young boy dumped water on my head.

Of course, what I experienced in school did not even compare to the injustices my parents suffered as children.

When my mother and father were young, people were imprisoned for believing in God.

Because America was seen as a Christian nation, Ukrainians looked down upon the country. People were constantly saying negative things about the United States, claiming it was definitely not the greatest nation on earth. Even my father's relatives did not support his idea of moving to America. No one really understood what America was like, and they feared the unknown.

However, my father didn't believe the anti-American propaganda. He thought it would be a wonderful place for our family to move—a place where our mother could get the medical assistance she needed for her head injury.

Papa would plead with our mother, "As soon as we get our visas, we'll go to America...you can get the help you need there. You can get well." But she refused.

"We are *not* moving to America," she would snap. "I refuse to move there. Everybody tells me it is a terrible place."

****

A few months later, Papa gave us the wonderful news: Our mother was finally coming home to us. My brothers and sisters and I rejoiced, clapping and hugging and laughing. We could not wait to see Mommy's beautiful face. Unfortunately, her homecoming was nothing like what we imagined.

Mother was not herself. She was like an empty shell, filled with pain and fear, sadness and anger. She was weak from sleepless nights and still tortured by agonizing headaches. She rarely smiled, and she no longer showed affection toward any of us.

We quickly learned that we should never argue with our mother or agitate her in any way. The slightest dispute would set her off, and she would launch into a fit of furious rage.

This was not our mother. It was as if we were living with a stranger.

Soon after Mommy returned home, her mother came over one afternoon to help out around the house. It was a warm, sunny day, and Babushka admired the blossoming flowers as she strolled up the paved walkway to our front door. She knocked at the door, but no one answered. She tried the knob and found that it was unlocked.

She poked her head in the door and shouted, "Hello?" Her voice echoed down the empty hallway.

Suddenly feeling a little concerned, Babushka rushed down the hall to the empty kitchen. "Hello? Is anyone home?"

As she walked past the door of my parents' bedroom, a shadowy shape caught her eye. My mother was sitting as still as a stone on the edge of the bed, wearing a heavy fur coat. She was staring off into space, her eyes glazed over, her face as emotionless as a mask.

"What are you doing wearing that winter coat, dear?" Babushka asked. "It's a perfectly warm day. Are you cold?"

Mother suddenly snapped out of her trance. For the first time, she noticed Babushka standing in the doorway. A look of confusion spread over her face as she shook off the fur coat.

****

One gorgeous spring evening, I went out to our garden to pick some flowers for my favorite teacher, Miss Alla Milanova. I adored Miss Milanova, even though she often confused me with my twin sister. She made Natasha and me sit in desks on opposite sides of the classroom so she could tell us apart.

Natasha and I both excelled at school, and Miss Milanova always told us how proud she was of us. It made me feel good about myself, and I took every opportunity to show my appreciation to her.

As I listened to the birds chirping and the bugs humming in our backyard, I carefully selected the most colorful, pristine blooms. A warm breeze ruffled my skirt and tousled my hair as I assembled the flowers into a perfect bouquet and tied a tiny pink ribbon around the stems. I could not wait to give it to Miss Milanova the next morning.

I was looking down and admiring the vibrant bouquet as I skipped back toward the house. I nearly ran smack into my mother, who was standing in the doorway.

"Oh, hi Mommy," I said, startled. "I didn't see you there."

Without any warning, she snatched the flowers from my hands and frantically tore them into a million pieces. Stunned into silence, I stood motionless and watched as she destroyed my beautiful bouquet.

After she demolished the flowers, Mother simply spun around on her heels and walked back into the house without a word. I stood there dumbfounded, staring down at the tiny torn petals and broken bits of stem on the ground. The sweet-smelling remnants whirled in the breeze before scattering across our backyard.

Later that night, Papa and Babushka came to our room to tuck us into bed.

"Goodnight, my dear children," Babushka said, as she shuffled around the room and kissed each of us on the cheek. "I'm headed home for the night." Babushka came over almost every day to help out around the house. She usually cooked dinner for us and tucked us into bed before catching the late train back to Kharkov.

When Babushka announced she was leaving, we all looked at Papa with fretful faces.

"Yes, Babushka is leaving for the night, but I'll be home from work early in the morning," Papa reassured us. Papa didn't like to leave our sick mother at home without another grownup around. But when he had to work the night shift at the factory, he didn't have much of a choice. Babushka blew us kisses from the doorway and said, "I'll see all of you soon." We listened to her footsteps fade as she walked down the hallway and out the front door.

"Papa?" Misha broke the silence. "What is it like in heaven?"

Papa grinned down at Misha and answered, "Well, it says in the Bible that the city in heaven is made out of gold, and the angels sing praises to God at all times." We all listened quietly, imagining this beautiful place. "It should be very peaceful and joyful, and people are like angels that can fly."

Papa pulled the blanket up to Misha's chin and sat down on the bed. He looked around the room at each of us and added, "You know, Jesus said the Kingdom of God belongs to children. Jesus always loved the children. In the Book of Matthew, He said, *'Let the little children come to me, and do not hinder them, for the kingdom of heaven belongs to such as these.'*" (Matthew 19:14) Papa stood up, gave each of us a tender kiss on the cheek and said, "Good night, my dear children. Sweet dreams." Then, he gently closed our bedroom door behind him.

A few minutes after Papa left the room, I told my brothers and sisters about Mother tearing up my bouquet. Alonna and Vera gasped in disbelief.

"That's so strange," Sasha said.

"Why would Mommy do such a terrible, mean thing?" Natasha whispered.

"Maybe she was upset about something else, and she just snapped," Sasha suggested. "You know how she gets when she has her headaches."

"Have you told Papa?" Misha asked.

"Yes, I told him," I answered. "He said I should go about my business and leave mother alone."

And with that, all of my brothers and sisters stopped talking—but I could tell from the sound of their breath that everyone was still awake. No one could sleep because we were all worrying about our mother.

Mommy had not gotten any better. If anything, she had gotten worse. Babushka knew it, I knew it, my brothers and sisters knew it...even Papa knew it. When I had told him about Mother destroying my flowers, I saw a dark cloud flash behind his eyes, like a thunderhead hovering over a sapphire sea.

Something was wrong with our mother....terribly wrong. And the very next day, it happened.

Chapter 5

The Unthinkable

A couple of years before my mother's accident, when Natasha and I started first grade, our teachers and classmates constantly confused the two of us. I tried to explain that I was the one with the tiny birthmark on my cheek, but it was too small for most people to notice.

One day after school, Natasha and I raced through the fence into our yard to find our mother scrubbing clothes. We did not have a washer or dryer, so Mommy washed all the clothes with her bare hands.

"Mommy, me and Tatyana don't want to wear the same clothes anymore," Natasha announced. Our mother looked up from the washboard, her green eyes glistening behind a weary face. A strand of damp hair fell across her forehead, and she tucked it behind her ear with a soapy hand.

"Our teacher can't tell us apart!" I explained.

"Oh," she sighed. "I guess that *is* a problem." She wiped her wet hands on her apron and then looked up at us again. "Okay, you can wear different clothes from now on. Now, go on and watch after your little brother and sisters."

"Oh, thank you Mommy!" I exclaimed as I wrapped my arms around her slumped shoulders. Natasha and I skipped into the house hand-in-hand as our mother returned to her laundry.

Even after Natasha and I stopped dressing alike, we remained inseparable. After all, we were twins. Sometimes I felt indelibly linked to her, as if we shared a single soul.

Natasha and I walked home from school together every single day, but we never ran out of things to talk about. During our two-mile stroll, we'd often discuss the future.

"Natasha," I asked one afternoon. "What kind of boy would you like to marry when you would grow up?"

"A very handsome one," she replied with a grin. I covered my mouth and giggled.

"Okay, what kind of wedding dress would you wear?" I asked. Natasha wrinkled her forehead as she thought about it. We passed the grocery store and barber shop and watched a handful of passengers spill out of the train station.

"I want a wedding dress just like the one mother wore," she finally answered. "And you?"

I kicked a pebble in the road and said, "I want one just like Aunt Inna's wedding dress." Inna was my mother's sister. "Or a very puffy, princess dress, covered with lots of flowers."

Natasha grinned. "That sounds pretty."

"How many children do you want to have?" I asked, as we walked past a fence. Two raven-haired boys were climbing a tree in the front yard.

"Oh, no more than five...definitely," she replied. "What about you?"

"I only want three," I answered. "No more than three!" Natasha laughed and grabbed my hand as we continued our walk home.

Although Natasha and I liked to imagine, we never could have guessed what the future actually held for us. All we knew for sure was that we loved each other and we had been blessed with a wonderful family. Like every other family, we had plenty of good times and plenty of bad times. Our mother and father struggled to take care of all of us. They managed to make it work, but their lives were certainly not easy.

But I didn't know just how hard life could be—until tragedy struck.

****

I still remember that day like it was yesterday. It was a bright, spring morning in 1989, a couple of weeks after my mother had returned home from Babushka's.

Like every other school day, my brothers, sisters and I rolled out of bed at dawn and quickly got dressed. But when we filed into the kitchen to eat breakfast, we were greeted by our unusually cheerful mother. I quickly realized this day wasn't going to be like every other day.

"Good morning, children!" Mommy sang as she pulled a bottle of milk out of the refrigerator. "I have a special surprise for you today."

We all looked at our mother with apprehensive faces. We never knew what to expect from her these days.

"No school today!" she announced. Sasha let out a "Woo-hoo!" Natasha and I beamed at each other as Alonna, Vera and Misha bounced up and down, clapping their little hands.

We weren't sure why Mommy was allowing us to stay home, but none of us dared to question her. For a fleeting moment, I wondered if she felt bad about destroying my bouquet the night before…or if she even remembered. Whatever the reason, I feared that if I uttered a single word it might ruin her wonderful mood. Anyway, we were all excited to stay home and play on such a beautiful day.

After breakfast, my mother had another surprise. Natasha and I were headed outside to play when we heard her padding down the attic stairs. She emerged from the doorway with an arm full of photo albums.

"Tatyana and Natasha, would you like to look at our old family photos?" she asked.

"Oh yes, mother! Please!" Natasha giggled, as she hopped from one foot to the other. "Will you turn the pages for us?"

"No, no, not today," she said, blowing a frizzy strand of hair out of her eye. "I was thinking you and Tatyana could look at the albums alone." My twin sister and I stood open-mouthed in disbelief. This was a truly special treat.

The family photo albums were typically off-limits to the children. The delicate, yellowing photos were glued to the album pages, and Mommy feared if they were handled too much, they may tear or fall off the page.

Usually, Mommy or Papa would hold the album in their lap and gently flip the pages as we children crowded around them, admiring the old photos. We were allowed to look but not touch. If any little fingers strayed near the pages, mother would slap them away and say, "Don't touch! You'll leave fingerprints."

But this day was different. "Come along, then," mother said, shuffling down the hallway with the albums carefully stacked in her arms. Natasha grabbed my hand, and we skipped after mother, through the kitchen and into our parents' bedroom.

"Here you go," she said as she sat the albums on her bedroom floor. Baby Julia cooed in her crib in the corner of my parents' room, shaking a rattle with her dimpled hand. "Have fun!" mother chirped, rushing out of the room.

"I can't believe it!" Natasha grinned, as she arranged the photo albums in a neat row on the floor. "I know," I whispered excitedly. I just couldn't get over my mother's unusual mood. She seemed calm and somewhat happier that morning.

"Maybe Mommy is finally feeling better," I said.

"I hope so," Natasha murmured as she flipped open a dark brown album.

"Look, it's Mommy when she was a little girl!" she exclaimed, pointing to a photo of a small toddler with a crown of chestnut curls.

"Aww, she was so cute," I said. "Where are the wedding pictures?"

"Here they are!" Natasha announced, holding up an ivory and gold album.

Our favorite photos were the wedding pictures of our parents. We loved to look at Mommy in her flowing white dress, her chocolate tresses delicately draped with a lacy veil. She was a strikingly beautiful bride.

The morning slipped away as Natasha and I flipped through album after album. After a while, baby Julia started to fuss. I lifted her from her crib and set her on the floor next to us. She crawled around the mountain of albums, and then collapsed onto the rug, kicking her chubby legs in the air with a gurgly giggle.

Natasha and I were in our own little world, completely mesmerized by the photos. We sniggered at snapshots of my father dressed in old-fashioned clothes as a little boy and marveled at photos of our mother when she was a stunning teenage girl. Nothing else in the world mattered to us—these photos of our family, these magnificent images forever frozen in time, had captured our undivided attention.

A couple of hours later, I glanced up at Natasha. "Do you hear that?"

Natasha looked up from a photo of my mother's sister, and stared at me wide-eyed. "What?"

"It's so quiet," I said. "It's *never* this quiet."

"The little ones must be playing outside," Natasha said, closing the album and placing it back on the stack. "At least they're not in here bothering us."

"Mommy might get mad if we don't keep an eye on them," I said. "Let's go see what they're up to." I scooped up baby Julia, now sound asleep with an empty bottle in her hand, and placed her back in her crib. We raced out of my parents' room and through the kitchen. As we entered the hallway, we found our mother closing the attic door behind her.

"Mommy," I said, "Where's Vera and Alonna and Mish-"

"I took them to your Grandma and Grandpa's house," she cut me off before I could finish my question.

Papa's parents, Grandma Veronica and Grandpa Michael, lived two miles away from us. For a split second, I thought it was a little odd that mother didn't ask Natasha and me if we wanted to go see our grandparents, too. But I decided she probably didn't want to interrupt us while we were looking at the photos. I didn't care too much, anyway. Natasha and I rarely had a chance to play together without having to watch over our three younger siblings.

"Come on, Tatyana," Natasha said, pulling at my arm. "Let's go look at some more photo albums. Last one to Mommy's room is a rotten egg!" she shouted, as she hurtled down the hall.

****

Later that morning, Natasha and I were still looking at the photos when we heard the front door slam shut. "Good morning!" Papa shouted from the front of the house. He'd just finished working the night shift at the factory. It was his last day at work before he would start his leave of absence to help mother at home.

Natasha and I raced into the kitchen to meet Papa, who was loaded down with two armfuls of groceries. "Well hello there, girls!" he sang as he set the grocery bags on the counter. "What are you doing home from school?"

"Mommy let us stay home today!" I answered happily.

"She did?" he responded, with a hint of concern in his voice. I saw his brow furrow slightly as he bent down to kiss each of us on the head. I guess he didn't want to question our mother's decisions, either.

"Well, I was hoping to get home sooner, but I got held up at the factory since it was my last day at work for a while. And speaking of, it's a good thing you're here...because today was pay day," he announced with a smile. "And I bought some kielbasa and rye bread for lunch!"

Papa always brought home something delicious to eat the day he got paid.

"Yummy, yummy in my tummy!" Natasha and I sang.

Mommy walked into the kitchen and gave our father a hug. "Good morning, dear," Papa said. "You look well today."

Mother flashed a shy grin as she began to put away the groceries.

"Where are the little ones?" Papa asked, glancing around the kitchen.

"I took them to your parents' house," Mommy answered, as she pulled rye bread from one of the bags.

"I see," Papa said cautiously. "Well, good. I bet my mother and father are happy to spend some time with them."

After a satisfying lunch, Natasha and I stood at the sink washing and drying dishes. Papa stood up from the table and stretched.

"Well, I think I'm going to go take a nap," he yawned as he strolled toward his bedroom. "It was a long night at work."

"I'm tired, too," Mother said. "I think I'll join you. Girls, you can go play outside when you're finished with the dishes."

"Okay, Mommy," Natasha said.

As she was walking out the kitchen, mother turned around and added in a quiet voice, "And don't go up to the attic. I don't want you playing up there today."

Natasha and I both turned and looked at her. I wasn't sure why she would ask us to stay out of the attic because we rarely played up there anyway. That room had always given me the creeps. All I knew is that I better agree with her. I didn't want to make her angry.

"Yes, Mommy," I answered. "We won't go up to the attic."

She nodded as she walked into her bedroom.

After we finished the dishes, Natasha and I skipped out into the sun-dappled backyard. We sat side-by-side in the soft grass, basking in the golden sun. We gathered daisies and made little wreaths out of them. When I finished braiding my daisies together, I placed the wreath on my head and looked up to discover Natasha was no longer sitting next to me. I found her half-made crown of daisies resting on the driveway. I thought it was strange that she did not finish her wreath, but I quickly forgot about it when we started a game of tag. We chased each other back and forth across the backyard.

We were picking berries from the garden when we saw our father walking out of our picket fence gate. "Where are you going, Papa?" I asked.

"Your mother has a headache," he said with a sigh. "I'm going to take the train to the pharmacy to get some medicine for her." He patted each of our heads before he strolled down the road toward the train station.

It made me sad to know that Mommy was having another one of her terrible headaches, especially after seeing how happy she'd been earlier that morning. Still, I held onto hope that she was getting better. Maybe her headaches would grow fewer and farther between until they eventually disappeared altogether.

Soon after Natasha and I went back inside, Sasha came home. He'd been out running some errands for Mommy. "Guess what I got?" he said with a smile, as he bounced into the kitchen. "Ice cream!"

Natasha and I squealed with delight, excited to enjoy a cold treat on such a warm day. But our little celebration was cut short when Mommy entered the kitchen. She looked pale and shaky, and I could tell she wasn't feeling well.

"Natasha, I need you to run an errand for me," she said.

"Okay, Mommy," Natasha said, sounding a little disappointed.

"We borrowed two liters of milk from the neighbors a few days ago," Mother said as she opened the refrigerator door. "I need you to take this to them to replace it." She handed a bottle of milk to Natasha, who quietly sauntered out of the room.

I felt bad for Natasha. She would have to walk all the way across the railroad to get to this neighbor's house. It would take her about half an hour to walk over there and back. I'm sure she was anxious to finish the errand so she could come home and eat her ice cream.

Mother turned to Sasha and said, "And I need you to get some things at the grocery store for me."

I knew Sasha had just returned from the store because that's where he'd bought the ice cream. But he didn't dare complain. We all knew it was not a good idea to argue with Mommy, especially when she had a headache.

After Natasha and Sasha left, Mother shuffled back to her bedroom, where baby Julia was napping. With Papa and all of the other kids gone, the house was unusually still. As I stood in the kitchen, I could hear the clock ticking on the wall.

I opened the freezer door and found the ice cream Sasha had bought. It was vanilla ice cream dipped in chocolate on a stick. My mouth watered as I pulled one from the box and unwrapped the frozen delicacy. I carefully carried the ice cream back to my bedroom, where I sat on the edge of the bed.

I gazed out the window as I licked the delicious chocolate covered ice cream. I saw our dog Reks pacing around the yard and sniffing at the air. I watched the green leaves rustle on the trees and spotted a couple of butterflies fluttering around some freshly blooming daffodils.

As I sat and admired the view, I savored each bite of that luscious, velvety ice cream. I was thinking about how joyful Mommy had been that morning, and I started to feel excited. "Our family is finally getting back to normal," I thought happily as I took another bite.

The next thing I knew, I heard my ice cream stick clatter to floor, and I felt an intense, burning pressure around my neck. I struggled to gasp for air. I suddenly realized someone was behind me, trying to choke me. I opened my eyes and strained to look over my shoulder. To my shock and disbelief, I saw my own mother's face hovering behind me. She had wrapped what felt like a small leather belt around my neck, and it was cutting off my airway. *My own mother was trying to suffocate me.*

I could not believe this was happening. I thought I must be dreaming or maybe Mommy was playing a joke on me. But when I realized I could not breathe, I knew this was no joke. If I wanted to live, I would have to fight for air. I started to thrash about on the bed. I kicked at my mother with my legs and tried to shove her away with my hands.

At one point, I managed to push her away from me, and I felt the pressure release from my neck. I gulped at the air and wheezed, "Mommy, what are you doing? Why are you..." But before I could finish, I felt the belt grip my neck, and I was fighting to catch my breath again. I could not understand what was happening. My mother did not utter a word. She seemed so calm and determined about whatever she was trying to do.

I kept shoving and kicking at her, until I felt the pressure release from my neck again. I saw my mother tumble off the bed and onto the floor.

In a state of confusion and fear, all I could think was that I needed to hide. Sometimes when we knew mother was coming to spank us, we would hide under the bed. But I knew that wouldn't work this time because she was right there on the floor, next to the bed.

I dashed across the room and squeezed into the small opening between the wall and our upright piano. I crouched down in that tiny, dusty space, my knees pulled to my chest, crying, "Mommy? Mommy? My Mommy?"

Not knowing what else to do, I called her name over and over. I still did not understand the seriousness of my situation. I kept thinking nothing else would happen. Mommy will leave me alone now. It's over. But if I had known what was coming, I would've leapt through the glass window to get away from her.

A few moments later, my mother started pulling the piano away from the wall, trying to get to me. The piano was very heavy, so she had to inch it away from the wall a little bit at a time and then claw at me with her hand. I wedged myself as far away from the opening as I could, struggling to escape her grasp. It was the most terrifying, nauseating moment of my life. I did not feel safe with my own mother, the person I most loved and trusted.

I soon realized my mother wasn't just grabbing at me with her fingers. She was holding a kitchen knife, and each time she swatted her hand behind the piano, she was grazing my legs, arms and neck with the sharp blade. She was trying to slit my throat and cut the arteries in my neck.

Eventually, either from the shock or the blood loss, I lost consciousness. One moment I was panting and staring terrified at the cobwebs clinging to the back of piano, waiting for my mother's knife-wielding hand to stab at me again, and the next moment the world spiraled out of view. Everything went dark, and I felt a sense of peace wash over me.

****

I awoke to a deafening ringing noise in my ears. When I tried to sit up, I realized I was curled up behind the piano in my bedroom. At first, I didn't understand how I'd gotten there. And suddenly, the visions of what had just happened came flooding back: my mother struggling on top of me, the belt around my neck. I remembered seeing her delicate hand grasping a knife, stabbing again and again into the dark space where I crouched behind the piano. I still had the sour taste of ice cream in my mouth, and I felt sick to my stomach. My throat burned, and my entire body ached. All I could think was, "I have to get out of here. I have to get out of the house."

I quietly slipped out from behind the piano and raced out of my bedroom. As I stumbled down the hallway and out the front door, I thought I heard someone screaming. Was I screaming? I wasn't sure. In my bewildered state, all I knew was I had to get away. I didn't know where to go or what would happen next.

As I tripped through our front yard, I felt weak and cold, and I was shaking all over. I was swallowed up by fear and confusion, like I was trapped in a nightmare. I kept thinking, "This isn't real. This isn't really happening." Real or not, I knew I had to get away. The only place I could think to go was the train station.

****

I staggered down the dirt road for what felt like hours. At some point, a woman walked up to me. "Oh my," she said, squatting down in front of me. "What happened to you, dear?"

"I...I...I tripped," I stammered. "I got hurt on a rock." She looked at me with frightened, sympathetic eyes, but I knew she didn't believe me.

I did not want to tell this woman what had really happened. I did not fully understand what had happened myself. All I knew is that I loved my Mommy, and I did not want her to get into trouble.

"Come with me," the woman said. She took my hand and led me to the grocery store.

I felt as if I were swimming through a dream. The bright lights in the grocery store were blinding, like a spotlight shining in my face. I stood swaying under the fluorescent glow, barely able to keep my balance. I could hear the woman speaking in hushed tones to a man who worked at the store. Shoppers stopped in their tracks, frozen with bags of potatoes and sausages dangling from their hands. They stared at me with looks of horror as the woman and the store clerk rushed me down the aisle to the bathroom.

The woman led me to the sink and turned on the faucet. When I looked into the mirror, I saw a ghastly face peering back at me. "Who is that?" I thought, completely baffled. I was shocked when I realized it was my own reflection.

I was barefoot and still wearing the dress I'd put on that morning, but it was tattered and blood-soaked. My neck, shoulders and arms were stained with crimson streaks, and the scarlet wounds in my neck glistened beneath the sterile bathroom lights. All the veins in my face bulged, and my eyes were so red, they appeared to be floating in blood. I could not comprehend what had happened to me. I did not even recognize myself.

After the woman helped me wash up at the sink, she led me back to the grocery store entrance. Some strangers I had never seen before picked me up in an unfamiliar car and drove me to the hospital.

Chapter 6

Hospital

Once I was in the hospital, I finally felt out of harm's way—but I was also weak and confused. I drifted in and out of consciousness, floating between the silhouettes of nurses moving against the bright hospital lights and an endless string of broken, jumbled dreams. Every now and then, I overheard the nurses speaking to one another in soft whispers: "She's only ten years old." "I know, it's just awful." "What do you think happened?"

When I awoke on a cold examination table, a friendly-faced doctor was standing over me. He kept asking what had happened to me, and I kept telling him the same story. "I tripped and fell on a rock," I whispered. "The rock cut me."

I vaguely remember the doctor stitching up my neck. I lay under the intensely bright lights, and all I could think about was my mother. I wasn't sure what had happened, but I knew she would get in trouble if anyone found out. "Dear God, please don't let them take my Mommy to jail," I silently prayed.

I was flooded with too many feelings at once, drowning in confusion. Although I didn't want the doctors and nurses to find out what had happened, the thought of going home to my mother terrified me. Every so often, the doctor would ask again what happened to me. I kept repeating the same answer. "It was a rock," I insisted. "I tripped and fell on a sharp rock."

When the doctor finished stitching up my neck, the nurses moved me to a hospital bed. Those kind nurses gently washed my entire body with a bucket of warm water, a soft washcloth and sweet-smelling soap. No one had ever taken care of me like that before. My mother was always busy caring for seven children, and I never felt that kind of tenderness from her. The special attention filled my heart with warmth, and I felt loved.

After they finished bathing me, the nurses told me to get some rest. They covered me in white cotton sheets that smelled faintly of bleach and left the room. Suddenly, I was all alone, blanketed in silence, no one talking or asking questions about what had happened.

As I lay in the hospital bed, staring at the cracked ceiling, the tears began to flow. I just lay there crying and crying, my cheeks soaked with salty wetness. I did not know what to think or feel because I did not understand what had happened. I just felt overcome with sorrow.

Later that evening, my father arrived. He rushed into my hospital room with a stern-looking police officer by his side. My heart leapt when I saw Papa's face, but my happiness was only momentary. Papa looked distraught, his eyes bloodshot and bewildered. I jumped from the hospital bed and ran into his arms. He hugged me tight, and we both cried hysterically.

"Papa, is Mommy okay? Is everyone okay?" I kept asking.

"Yes, Tatyana," he choked back tears. "Everyone is fine. It's going to be okay."

"Where is everyone?" I peered over Papa's shoulder, half expecting to see my brothers and sisters in the hallway.

"Sasha is in the waiting room," he said. Then, after a brief pause he added, "Your mother and the rest of your siblings went to stay with Aunt Larissa for a little while." Aunt Larissa, one of my mother's sisters, lived hours away in Nikolayev, a city near the Black Sea. I was puzzled as to why they would go there, but Papa assured me I would see them soon.

"Now, Tatyana," he said, pulling away from me so he could look into my eyes. He gently gripped my shoulders with his big hands. "You must tell this police officer the truth about what happened to you."

I remained silent as I glanced over at the grim-faced officer and back to my father's pleading eyes. After a few moments of deafening silence, I looked down at the tile floor and muttered, "I fell on a rock. The rock cut me."

"Honey, we know that's not true," Papa said softly, as he wrung his calloused hands and glanced nervously around the room. Then, he looked straight into my face, practically piercing my soul with his sky blue gaze and said firmly, "Tatyana, you *must* tell this officer the *truth*."

By the tone of Papa's voice and the fear in his eyes, I knew something was very serious. But I was still terrified to tell them what my mother had done.

Finally, I looked at the police officer and said, "I will tell you what happened if you *promise* not to take my Mommy to jail."

The officer glanced at my father and then looked back at me, staring straight into my eyes. "Okay, Tatyana," he said. "I promise."

"Sir, our mother is very, very sick," I began. And then I told my father and the police officer everything. I told them about the ice cream and Mommy jumping on me. I told them about the leather belt and the struggle on the bed. I told them about hiding behind the piano, the knife stabbing at me until I fainted, and how I escaped from the house.

As I recounted my story, Papa just sat there listening, tears streaming down his face. He did not utter a word. The police officer furiously scribbled notes on a pad, and every now and then I saw something like shock or disgust creep over his face. When I finished my story, the officer patted me on the head, thanked us and left the room. Papa stood up and walked over to me. He sat on the edge of my hospital bed and pulled me close to him.

My father stayed by my side all through the night. He kept hugging me and telling me that everything was going to be okay. I believed him, and I felt safe in his arms. He held me tight until I finally drifted off into a dreamless sleep.

****

For the next week and a half, I slowly recovered in the hospital. I spent my days chatting with Papa and my big brother Sasha, reading books and watching cartoons. We did not have a television set at home, so watching anything on TV was a real treat. The silly cartoons helped me escape from reality for a little while. They took my mind off what had happened, and every now and then I'd catch myself quietly laughing.

A few people came to see me while I was in the hospital, but Papa was very choosy about who could visit. I overheard him telling the nurses he didn't want visitors coming and going because he thought it would be too stressful for me.

One day, my favorite teacher, Miss Alla Milanova, appeared at the door of my hospital room. I thought I was dreaming when I first saw her beaming face. I was thrilled to see her, and she brought me a special treat. It was chocolate spreadable butter, and it was the most delicious food I had ever put in my mouth. Unfortunately, I had lost my appetite since the incident with my mother, so I could only handle a few bites.

"Aren't you going to eat more?" Miss Alla asked.

"It's so yummy," I answered shyly. "But I'll save the rest for later."

After Miss Alla gave me the chocolate butter, I suddenly remembered the gift I never had the chance to give her. The beautiful bouquet of flowers I had carefully picked for her—the one my mother destroyed the night before she attacked me. I imagined the dried out, brown petals still swirling around in my backyard, and I felt heartbroken.

When my eyes filled with tears, Miss Alla asked me what was wrong. I told her about the flowers—but not the part about my mother destroying them. I just told her I had dropped the bouquet. I did not want her to think my mother was a terrible person.

"Oh, Tatyana," Miss Alla said through a tearful voice. "Don't you worry about that now." She hugged me close, and I breathed in her honeysuckle scent. The sweet smell reminded me of my mother, and my heart fluttered. "I'm so very proud of you," she said. "You are such a good, smart girl. I'm so glad you are okay."

Papa took extra special care of me while I was in the hospital. For the first time I could remember, I had his undivided attention. He brought me fresh, brilliantly colored fruits and vegetables, and he took me for walks outside on the hospital grounds.

During our walks, I would ask him if Mommy and my siblings were alright. He kept assuring me that everyone was okay and we would see them soon.

"Will you please tell Mommy that I forgive her?" I would ask him over and over. "Please, Papa?" He would just nod, his troubled eyes glistening.

I detected the sadness on my father's face, and I could tell he was struggling to stay strong. I wasn't sure if he was just worried about me or if he missed my mother and siblings, too. I had the feeling he was hiding something, but I couldn't quite put my finger on it.

Every now and then, a sense of uncertainty would creep into my heart. I would start thinking something was horribly wrong. But I would immediately push those anxious feelings away.

I had so much hope that everything would be okay as soon as we reunited with the rest of our family. I couldn't wait to see my mother, hug her and tell her I had forgiven her. I missed my younger brother and sisters terribly, and I felt like I was missing a piece of my soul without Natasha by my side.

Then the day finally arrived. One bright spring morning, Papa told me it was time to leave the hospital. I thought I would burst with happiness. I was so excited to finally see my family, go back to school and get on with my life.

After we gathered my things, we climbed into Papa's car. As he pulled out of the hospital parking lot, he said, "We're going to live with Grandma Veronica and Grandpa Michael for a little while, okay?" Papa's parents lived two miles away from us, and I was a little confused as to why we couldn't just go home.

"Will Mama and Natasha and the rest of them be there?" I asked expectantly.

"Sasha is there," Papa answered hesitantly as he rubbed his forehead. "But the rest of your siblings and your mother are going to stay with Aunt Larissa for a while longer."

My heart sank, but I didn't question my father. I figured he knew what was best for us right now. I just hoped and prayed the rest of my family would come home soon.

I watched as the city of Kharkov faded away and eventually disappeared from our rearview mirror. And before I knew it, we were driving down the dirt road to my grandparents' house. I gazed out the car window, and was surprised to see wilted tulips strewn across the ground. The beautiful flowers were scattered along the side road for at least two or three miles. They looked brown and limp, like they'd been sitting in the sun for quite a while.

"Papa, why are there flowers on the ground everywhere?" I asked. He did not answer me. He just kept his eyes on the road until we finally pulled into my grandparents' driveway. I felt that nagging sense of worry creep in again.

****

When we arrived at Grandma and Grandpa's house, they were waiting in the yard with Sasha. They all hugged me tight and said they were happy I was feeling better.

My grandparents lived on a farm. They had cows, pigs and chickens, and they grew tulips to sell at the local market. I always had fun visiting their farm, but after a few days of living there, I quickly grew bored. A week after we left the hospital, I told Papa I was ready to go back to school.

"Tatyana, you cannot go back to school yet," Papa answered.

I did not understand, and I was very frustrated. I missed Miss Alla, and I was tired of spending every day on the farm.

The next morning, I was determined to go back to school anyway. As soon as the sun's first rays peeked over the horizon, I threw on some clothes and tiptoed out the sunroom door. I rushed down the driveway, heading toward the dirt road that led to my school.

"Tatyana, where are you going?" I suddenly heard Sasha shout from the front yard.

"I'm going to school…and you can't stop me!" I yelled without even glancing over my shoulder. I took off running, but Sasha caught up with me and grabbed me by my arm. As I struggled to break free, Grandma Veronica burst through the front door.

"Tatyana, get back in this house!" she said sternly as she trotted across the front yard. "You cannot go to school today."

I wriggled out of Sasha's grasp, but Grandma and Sasha blocked my way to the end of the driveway.

"Get out of my way!" I screeched, feeling the anger bubble up in my chest. When they stood their ground, I reached up and slapped Sasha on his cheek.

"Ow!" Sasha bellowed. He rubbed at his face where a small, cherry red handprint was quickly forming. "Why'd you do that?"

Grandma grabbed me by the arm and marched me back into the house. When she told my father what had happened, he breathed a heavy sigh.

"Tatyana, what were you thinking?" he asked.

"I just don't understand why I can't go back to school!" I sniffled as tears ran down my cheeks.

"Tatyana," Papa said, wrapping an arm around my shoulder. "You cannot go to school because you missed too many days while you were sick. Your teacher told me you'll have to wait until next year to go back."

I was crushed, but I believed my father. I just couldn't comprehend all the changes that were happening in my life.

"Things will get better, Tatyana," Papa said. "I promise."

I spent the next few months looking for ways to stay busy on my grandparents' farm. I walked with Sasha and my Uncle Andrey when they took the cows to graze in nearby fields. While the cows ambled through the pasture and nibbled grass, I picked wild strawberries and played games with my brother and uncle. Sasha and Uncle Andrey were always kind to me—even when I provoked and annoyed them. They knew I had been through a traumatic experience, and they didn't want to upset me.

I helped Grandma plant flowers and vegetables. Sometimes, I just sat in the yard and watched as she and Grandpa worked on the farm. I even made friends with a few of the children in the neighborhood.

I enjoyed living with my grandparents—but the entire time, I was waiting patiently to see the rest of my family. Whenever I would ask my father when they were coming home, he would explain that mother was still recovering at my aunt's house. He said my Aunt Larissa was taking good care of Mommy and my brother and sisters. I believed him, but I was anxious to see them again.

One afternoon, I walked into my grandparents' sunroom and spotted Grandpa doing something very strange. He was holding a rolled newspaper in his hand, and one end of it had caught on fire. As my grandpa raced around the kitchen like a madman, he waved the flaming newspaper around, filling the entire house with smoke.

"Grandpa is trying to burn down the house!" I thought in silent horror, and I raced out of the house as fast as I could. As I stood in the yard waiting for the house to go up in blazes, nothing happened. I waited there, just watching, for a very long time. Still, nothing happened.

Finally, I crept back up to the house and poked my head through the door. My grandpa was sitting at the table eating lunch, acting as if nothing was wrong.

"G-g-grandpa?" I stammered, filled with fear. "What were you doing with that n-n-newspaper on fire?"

He looked up from his lunch and smiled at me. "Oh, that's how I shoo away the flies," he said with a laugh. "They don't like the smoke. You want some lunch?"

I felt my fear melt away, and I was so relieved that everything was okay.

In the months after my mother attacked me, I experienced many moments of sheer terror like this. I had a hard time trusting anyone—even my own father. When I misbehaved and my father yelled at me, I would tremble with dread. Papa had to figure out ways to discipline me that would not paralyze me with fear.

Another day, I was playing in the yard when my Grandma opened the front door. "Tatyana," she called, "I have a special treat for you!"

"Oh, goodie!" I sang as I dashed inside the house. When I ran into the kitchen, I found Grandma standing at the counter, holding a chocolate dipped ice cream treat on a stick.

The memories came rushing back: the sound of the ice cream stick clattering to the floor—waking up behind our upright piano with that sour taste in my mouth.

Grandma Veronica stood there with a baffled look, waiting for me to take the ice cream. Grabbing my stomach with one hand and covering my mouth with the other, I raced out of the house just in time to retch all over the back steps.

****

A few months after we moved in with my grandparents, I was settling down for an afternoon nap. As Papa covered me with a blanket, I could see sorrow swimming behind his eyes.

"Tatyana, I have something to tell you," he said quietly, as he lay down next to me. I saw his blue eyes darken with sadness, and I could tell whatever he was about to say was excruciating for him. I touched his arm gently with my hand.

"Your mother and brother and sisters..." He paused, taking a deep, shuddering breath. "Your mother and your siblings are never coming back."

My hand fell away from his arm. I just lay there staring at Papa, shocked into silence. "The day that your mother—when she—tried to hurt you..." He wrestled with the words. "You and Sasha were the only ones who survived. Natasha, Misha, Vera, Alonna and Julia—they all passed away."

My head started to spin violently, and I felt like I was losing my footing on a wobbly tightrope. All along, I thought this tragedy had happened only to me. I thought I was the only one mother had tried to harm. But now I realized that my mother was not just trying to hurt me that day—she was trying to *kill* me. And she *had* killed my siblings.

I reluctantly started to piece together the unspeakable events from that terrible day, and it all became horribly clear. Misha, Vera and Alonna had never gone to visit my grandparents. While Natasha and I were busy looking at the photo albums that morning, our mother had killed them in the attic, probably strangling each of them with a leather belt—the same way I was supposed to die. *"Don't go up to the attic,"* my mother's words echoed in my mind. *"I don't want you playing up there today."* She must have killed sweet baby Julia later—maybe even while Natasha and I were playing outside, after Papa left for the pharmacy. The thought made me sick with grief. Then, when Mommy sent Sasha and Natasha off on their errands, she had tried to kill me.

"But…but what about Mommy?" I asked, almost afraid to hear the answer. "Where is Mommy now?"

"Tatyana," Papa said, with tears streaming down his face. "Your mother is also dead. She…she killed her-…she committed suicide."

My soul slipped off that shaky tightrope and plunged into the darkness. I felt like I was falling farther and farther away as Papa continued.

He explained that as Sasha was leaving the grocery store that day, he saw a little girl who looked like me. She was covered in blood, and some strangers were placing her in the backseat of a car. Sasha thought surely this couldn't be Tatyana—but when he came closer he realized it *was* me.

"Tatyana!" he shouted at me through the car window, but I didn't respond. I was slumped over in the backseat, completely unconscious. "What happened?!" Sasha frantically looked around at the strangers surrounding the car. "Where are you taking my sister?"

"You're her brother?" one of the men asked Sasha. Sasha nodded as tears began to sting at his eyes. When he saw the car pulling away, he tried to race after it. The man grabbed Sasha by the shoulder. "Hey, wait! We don't know what happened—a woman found her bleeding on the side of the road. They're taking her to the hospital. You need to tell your parents. Go get your parents!"

Sasha jumped on his bike and raced home. He ran to the front of the house and peered through the windows, fearing there could be burglars inside. He thought someone might have broken into the house and attacked me. He knocked on the glass, but he saw no movement. The house was eerily still and silent.

Sasha then noticed that the front door was partially opened. As he walked through the door, he felt a chill run through his body. He sensed some sort of evil presence looming in our home. He walked down the hallway to our bedroom, and that's when he saw a terrible sight: Natasha's motionless, bloody body sprawled across the bed.

"Natasha?" he said, as he touched her limp arm. She felt cold. Fear took a hold of him, and he knew he had to get out of the house. He dashed out the front door and ran all the way to the railroad station, where he called the police. He was crying hysterically, and people began to gather around him asking him questions. One of our distant relatives recognized Sasha, and she gave him a valium from her purse to calm him down.

When Papa returned home from the pharmacy, he saw police officers swarming through our yard. He dashed up to our front door when a man in uniform stopped him and told Papa the horrific news: They had just found his wife's body along with his five lifeless children, Misha, Vera, Alonna, Natasha and baby Julia. Overcome with despair, Papa let out a spine-tingling wail. He furiously screamed and cried. A police officer had to give him a shot in his arm to pacify him.

The police later told Papa they discovered a tank of gasoline my Mother had prepared—she had planned to burn down the house. They said that probably, when she realized I had escaped, she feared I would call the police. There was no time for her to start a fire. So instead, my mother went to the attic and committed suicide.

"If she had burned down the house," Papa said, between sobs, "the evidence would have been destroyed—and they probably would have accused *me* of the murders. If you had not survived, if….if you had not told that police officer in the hospital what happened, I would've gone to jail."

As Papa told me all of this, I was absolutely speechless—I could not find words. I just lay there on the bed next to my father and cried. I felt like I was choking on agony. For a split second, I thought I would lose consciousness.

And suddenly, another horrific memory rushed into my head. As I escaped from the house that day, I had heard someone screaming—a voice crying for help. And now, I remembered: It was Natasha.

She must have returned from running her errand while I was unconscious behind the piano. When I was sneaking out of the house, my mother was murdering my twin sister.

I had escaped from the house without helping Natasha. Anger and guilt coursed through my veins.

"I didn't save her!" I shrieked through my sobs. "My poor Natasha—I left without her!!"

"Oh, no Tatyana…you were hurt and confused," my father tried to explain. "You did not understand what was happening. Even if you did, you were injured and too weak to help your sister."

Papa continued talking, but his words sounded muffled. I felt myself tumbling deeper and deeper into a bottomless pit of sorrow. My brother and sisters, my mother—they were gone. Never again would I hold Natasha's hand as we walked home from school chatting about our future. Never again would I see Misha dress up in a silly groom's costume or listen to Vera and Alonna's girlish giggles. Never again would I feel baby Julia's dimpled hand wrap around my finger. And never again would I inhale the sweet scent of my mother's chocolate tresses.

I sobbed and sobbed until I wilted with exhaustion. Weak from crying, I leaned my head against my father's chest.

"Remember the tulips you saw on the road on the way home from the hospital?" Papa asked, holding me close and wiping the tears from my cheeks. "Those were from the funeral procession for your siblings and mother. They were Grandma and Grandpa's tulips, grown right here on this farm."

I remained silent. I had no words. I trembled in his arms as the tears kept falling.

"We will see them again one day, Tatyana," Papa soothed as he held me tight. "We'll see them again in heaven."

Chapter 7

The Trip

I walked around in a fog for the next few days. I sobbed until I had no tears left to cry. When my tears ran dry, I just lay in the bed staring at the ceiling, feeling as if my heart was breaking into a million pieces in my small chest. Papa, Sasha and I prayed for strength day after day—but I could not find the strength.

I felt as weak and lifeless as broken-winged bird. I was only ten years old, and I had lost my mother, my twin sister, my three little sisters and my younger brother. It was too much to bear.

One crisp autumn day, I drifted into my grandparent's backyard. I collapsed onto the grass, soaking up the rays from an orange sun. As I lay there, staring up into a cloudless sky, I suddenly felt a sense of peace. I imagined that somewhere far beyond that indigo sky, in a beautiful hidden land, Natasha, Misha, Vera, Alonna and even baby Julia were happily running and jumping, bounding through fields and gardens with beaming faces. I thought about that joyful golden city in heaven Papa had described to us. I wanted to be there with them—I missed them so much it hurt. I would do anything to be with my dear siblings again.

After that day, I slowly started to accept reality. I finally realized that no matter how many tears I cried, I could not bring them back. My mother, brother and sisters were gone from this world forever, and I had to learn to live with that. I clung onto the thought that I would join them in heaven one day. That one tiny ray of hope kept me going.

Papa tried his best to distract me so I wouldn't dwell on the past. He struggled to find little projects and adventures to keep me occupied. Some days, he would take me to the store and let me pick out dolls, something I had never been able to do before.

Suddenly, I was the center of Papa's attention, and I kind of enjoyed it. It helped me heal, little by little. I could feel the pieces of my heart slowly mending, as if Papa were sewing them back together into a crooked patchwork. But my father was running out of diversions on my grandparents' small farm. That's when he decided it was time to embark on a journey.

While I was in the hospital recovering, Papa had sold our house and all of our belongings. He got rid of every object that reminded him of our family's terrible tragedy. He gave our dog Reks to a neighbor and threw out all of our family photo albums—as if tossing those images might erase our catastrophic past. My father may have acted impulsively, but he was blinded by sadness and anger, too traumatized to think things through. His heart was broken, and he wanted to wipe out the horrific memories.

He made a decent profit on the sale of the house, and for once in our lives we had some extra money. And Papa was ready to spend it.

One afternoon, Papa burst into kitchen, where Sasha and I were eating bacon and eggs for breakfast. "Tatyana, Sasha—pack your things," he said with a smile, his sky blue eyes shining. "We're going on a trip!"

Sasha and I leapt from our seats, clapping and laughing with excitement. I could not wait to leave the farm for a little while, to get away from this town and escape the memories that haunted me.

"Where are we going, Papa?" I asked, my mind racing with possibilities.

"We're going to the beach in Gruzia!" he announced. "Our plane leaves tomorrow, so we need to start packing right away."

"Our PLANE?" I gasped, and looked at Sasha whose jaw had dropped to his chest. We had never flown on a plane before, and I was overcome with nervous anticipation.

The next day, I found myself rushing through the crowded Kharkov airport alongside Papa and Sasha. I was amazed by the hustle and bustle of the hundreds of travelers heading to exotic places all over the world.

We boarded our plane to Gruzia, which Americans call Georgia. I gripped onto the armrests of my seat and felt my stomach drop as our plane took off. I peered out my tiny airplane window, watching the people, cars and buildings grow smaller and smaller until they disappeared altogether.

As we flew above a white blanket of clouds, the apricot sun filled the airplane cabin with golden light. I gazed out at the topaz sky stretching on as far as my eyes could see, hoping to catch a glimpse of heaven. And suddenly I thought I heard my siblings' quiet whispers and giggles, as if they were sitting right next to me.

When we arrived in Gruzia, a friend of my Papa's picked us up at the airport. As he drove us to his house near the beach, I thought I might explode with excitement. I had never seen the Black Sea before, and I couldn't wait to dip my toes in the water.

I realized that Papa's friend was very rich when we pulled into a driveway curling up to an enormous estate. The family grew roses for a living, and their house was surrounded by gorgeous gardens bursting with the vibrant, sweet-smelling blooms.

"Well, what do you think, Tatyana?" Papa asked as I admired the gorgeous house through the car windows. I looked at him with wide eyes. "This is where we'll be staying during our vacation," he said with a grin. "Do you think it will do?"

Papa's friend laughed, and I shyly responded, "Yes, Papa. It's…beautiful."

When Sasha and I stepped out of the car, we were greeted by the man's wife and their four children.

"Come on," said a little boy with a mop of blonde hair. He grabbed my hand and announced, "I want to show you my room!"

Sasha and I quickly made friends with the children. They shared their toys and games with us, and we played together and told each other funny stories. But we didn't dare tell them about our family's tragedy. It was an unspoken secret—a rough grain of sadness quietly scraping at our souls.

Later that day, Papa took us to the beach. When my feet touched the soft sand, I looked up and could barely believe my eyes. I took in a glorious expanse of rolling waves, the dark blue water stretching out to a perfectly straight line along the horizon. I was so struck by the beauty of it that I stood motionless on the beach, taking it all in.

"Well, what are you waiting for?" Papa said. "Let's go swimming!"

Sasha and I raced to the edge of the surf, and I stuck my toes in the Black Sea's foamy, warm waters.

"Come on, Tatyana, it feels great!" Sasha laughed as he rushed out into the water until it was up to his chest.

I nervously waded out after him, scanning the water for any movement beneath the surface. I had read about jellyfish, and I was terrified that I would get stung. "Come on, scaredy cat!" Sasha shouted. When he splashed me, I could taste the saltiness on my tongue. I had never tasted salt water before.

We spent the rest of the afternoon splashing in the surf, collecting sea shells and building castles in the sand. Papa tried to teach me how to swim in the gentle waves, holding me in his strong arms, telling me to "Kick, kick, kick!" Although I was afraid of the crashing water and stinging sea creatures, I basked in my father's attention.

For the next few weeks, we played at the beach every day and returned to the rich family's house every evening. After dinner, Papa and I would stroll through their expansive rose gardens, just as the sun was starting to set. I would gently run my hand along the silky red, yellow and pink petals, breathing in their sweet perfume. I had never seen anything like it in my life. I felt like I was in heaven.

I imagined the beautiful crowns Natasha and I could make from these lovely roses, and my heart ached with longing for my dear twin sister. I suddenly remembered that on the day of the terrible tragedy, she had never finished her final crown of flowers in our backyard. I wondered if she had flowers to pick in heaven. I wondered if she missed me as much as I missed her.

****

Soon after we returned to Grandma and Grandpa's farm, Papa had another surprise for us. "We're moving to America!" he shouted one evening as he burst in the family room waving a large envelope in the air. "Our U.S. visas are finally here!"

Sasha and I both stared at Papa with wide eyes, and Grandma Veronica immediately burst into tears. "Oh, Mother," Papa said. "I know it's far away, but we need a fresh start."

"I know, you're right," she answered, choked with sobs. "I'm just going to miss all of you so very much."

Of course, not all of our family members were so supportive of Papa's decision to move to America. But my father did not care. He was determined to leave our country, put our tragic past behind us and start over in a new home. So, we slowly began to pack our things. We would begin our long journey just a few weeks later. Sasha and I were not as excited as our father, but we figured he knew what was best for our family.

"Are you excited about going to America?" Papa asked me one morning as I stuffed some clothes in a leather suitcase.

"No, Papa," I whispered, tears brimming behind my eyes. "I'm scared." The thought of leaving my grandparents behind and moving to another country made me feel anxious and uncertain.

"Don't be afraid, Tatyana," Papa said, taking me into his arms. "It will be a great adventure. And we won't be going to America right away."

"We're not? Where are we going?" I asked, leaning my head into his chest.

He stroked my hair and said, "First, we'll go to Vienna for a few weeks. Then we'll head to Italy, and we'll stay there for a while. And then, we'll fly to America. Doesn't that sound exciting?"

A tear dripped off my chin and fell onto Papa's arm. "No…it sounds scary," I sighed.

"Oh, Tatyana…there's nothing scary about it! You'll see. And I'll be with you the whole time." He rocked me back and forth in his lap like a baby. "It's just you, Sasha and me now. We'll always have each other."

Before we knew it, the day had arrived. Papa, Sasha and I stood in the busy Kharkov train station surrounded by family members and church friends. Everyone was crying, not knowing what would happen to us, unsure if they would ever see us again.

I tried to stay strong, but then Grandma Veronica walked up to me to say goodbye. She had tears streaming down her wrinkled cheeks, and when she took me in her arms, I burst into tears. I loved her so much. I had spent so much time with my dear Grandma, and she was like a mother to me.

As Papa pulled me away from Grandma and said, "It's time to go, Tatyana," I felt like my heart was being ripped from my chest. The thought of losing another family member was too much to bear, and I sobbed uncontrollably as Sasha, Papa and I boarded the train.

It was a sad farewell. We waved from the window to Grandma and Grandpa and our weeping church friends as the train whistle blew. The train picked up speed, and I watched our family and friends fade away until I could no longer see them. It was just Sasha, Papa and me now. Just the three of us.

****

Our first stop was Vienna, an absolutely stunning place. I had never seen such a clean, pristine city. At the hotel, we met other Russian families who were also immigrants headed for America. When we learned that they were Christian like us, we came together to pray and worship. It was the first time I could remember being so free and open with our religion, and it felt wonderful. I started to feel more comfortable in this new country—but we did not stay for long. A few weeks later, we boarded a train for Italy.

Our stay in Italy was amazing. We visited countless historical places, took in the beautiful scenery and marveled at tourists from around the world. My father took us to Rome to visit the Vatican, and I was in awe. We went to the flea market every weekend and admired all the elaborate items people were buying and selling. I was fascinated with the Italian people who were so full of life and loved to eat such delicious food.

We found a Russian community filled with immigrants like us, all trying to get to America. We made many friends. I met some Russian and Ukrainian girls my age, and we played games and told each other stories. But I knew not to talk about my family's tragedy. I was to keep that a secret, locked away in the depths of my heart—a jagged grain chafing away at my aching soul.

"It is our family's secret," Papa would say. "No one else needs to know."

Still, some of the other immigrants somehow found out about our tragedy. But when they brought it up, we refused to talk about it. Papa thought it would be best for our family to keep it to ourselves. He was trying to protect us from reliving the tragedy because he feared it would destroy us. Papa was trying not to dwell on the past—he wanted all of us to move forward with our lives.

Although I made friends in Italy, I also spent a lot of time alone. At night, I wept into my pillow until I grew weak with exhaustion and drifted off to sleep. Sometimes, I would dream that my mother, brother and sisters were in Italy with us, and it seemed so real. But then I'd jerk awake and remember they were gone—and the tears would flow again.

In Italy, there were enough Russian and Ukrainian people to hold an actual church service. Papa, Sasha and I went to church every Sunday and worshiped with the other immigrants. My father also began to preach again. Even though he had suffered from such a horrific tragedy, Papa never grew bitter with God, and he took every opportunity to praise Him.

One day, I found Papa reading the Bible in our hotel room.

"Papa?" I said.

He looked up from the Bible, his finger holding his place. "Yes?"

"Do you ever get…angry? About—you know. What happened to us?"

He patted the bed, signaling me to sit. I plopped down next to Papa, and he wrapped his arm around my shoulder.

"No, Tatyana," he said in a serious voice. "I am not angry…at God or anyone else." He paused and looked down at me. "Have you ever heard the Bible story about Job?"

I nodded, and looked up into his blue eyes.

"Then, you might remember that Job was a righteous man who had many tragedies in his life. He lost all of his children and everything he owned—but he *never* grew angry with God. Even after he lost everything, Job said, 'Naked I came from my mother's womb, and naked I will depart. The Lord gave and the Lord has taken away; may the name of the Lord be praised.'(Job 1:21) I know I am not as righteous of a man as Job, but I am inspired by him. That's why I choose to not be angry. I choose to humble myself before God."

I smiled up at Papa's face, and he kissed me on the forehead. I felt very proud of Papa in that moment. He seemed so strong, so determined. I started to think maybe I should stop being angry and sad, too. But it was so hard.

"Tatyana," he said, patting my arm. "I know we have a lot of unanswered questions. But we have to learn how to live with them. And if we stay strong and keep praying, we're going to be okay. God will take care of us... and we will take care of each other."

****

After three wonderful months in Italy, it was time to say goodbye yet again. We embraced our new friends, kissed their tear-streaked cheeks and wished them the best. Then, Papa, Sasha and I boarded a plane for our final destination: America.

During the long flight, I gazed out my airplane window thinking about the friends and family we were leaving behind. I drifted in and out of sleep until the pilot came on the loud speaker and announced that we were beginning our approach into New York. I felt a mixture of excitement and anxiety race through my veins.

As our plane emerged from the hazy fog, I was mesmerized by the sprawling city below. There were twinkling lights, towering buildings and an endless stream of cars as far as my eye could see.

After our plane landed, we walked down a long, dark hallway before entering the brightly lit airport. Sasha pointed to a mass of smiling, waving people who were waiting for their family members and friends to arrive. Amid the crowd, I spotted a kind looking woman and her excited family holding up a huge banner with the words, "Welcome to America" in Russian. It was our sponsor, Mrs. Rose.

"Oh, that is so nice," Papa remarked. "She wrote it in Russian!"

We raced up to meet Mrs. Rose and the rest of her family, and they warmly greeted us with hellos, hugs and handshakes. After meeting them, I knew that we were in good hands. I felt safe.

Mrs. Rose and her family lived in upstate New York, and they had learned about us through their church. They had agreed to take us in until we could find a home of our own. I thought it took a very special family to invite strangers from another country into their home. After Mrs. Rose picked us up from the airport, she drove us to her lovely home, where she had prepared a dinner of traditional Ukrainian food for us. We were very surprised and grateful for her thoughtfulness and hospitality.

The Rose family was Christian, so we bonded with them quickly. But because Papa, Sasha and I did not speak any English, we struggled to break through the language barrier. We used a Russian/English dictionary to communicate with the Roses and other Americans. It was stressful, but it kept our minds busy so we did not have time to dwell on the past.

One day, Mrs. Rose strolled into the family room, where I was sitting on the couch studying my language dictionary.

"Tatyana?" she asked with a friendly smile.

"Yes?" I answered in English.

"How would you like to go shopping?"

Not certain what she was saying, I stared at her for a few moments before flipping through the pages of my dictionary to find the word, "shopping." With my finger still holding the spot on the page, I looked back up and nodded at Mrs. Rose, a huge smile breaking across my face.

"Okay, let's go!" she said, clapping her hands and beaming from ear to ear.

Mrs. Rose took me to a store called JCPenney at the nearby mall. I had never been to a mall before, and when we entered the massive department store, I couldn't believe my eyes.

Bathed in bright yellow lights, there was a perfume counter filled with glittering glass containers, an entire section overflowing with boots, high heels and other shoes, and an endless sea of jewelry cases shimmering with sparkly earrings, necklaces and bracelets. And directly in front of us, there was an enormous room, as big as our entire house in Lubotin, brimming with girl's shirts, skirts, pants and dresses of every shape, color, size and pattern you could imagine. I had never seen anything like it before. I thought I was dreaming.

"Go ahead, Tatyana," Mrs. Rose said, giving me a little nudge. "Pick out an outfit for yourself."

I whisked around and looked at her with wide eyes. "Yes?" was all I could manage.

"Yes, choose whatever you'd like!" Mrs. Rose said with a laugh. "It's my treat."

After roaming through the rows of clothes, running my hands along the different fabrics, my eyes were drawn to the calming pastel colors of a lovely Easter dress. It was a beautiful white dress covered with pale blue, pink and green flowers.

When Mrs. Rose caught me admiring the garment, she grabbed it off the rack and rushed me off to the dressing room with a girlish giggle. I slipped on the dress and tied the ribbon in the back. It fit perfectly. When I walked out of the dressing room, Mrs. Rose let out a gasp. "Oh, Tatyana! You look stunning."

I stood in front of the three-way mirror and shyly glanced at my reflection. I couldn't believe my eyes. I felt beautiful.

"We have to buy you some new shoes to go with it!" Mrs. Rose exclaimed.

As Mrs. Rose paid for the dress and white patent leather shoes at the customer service desk, I grabbed her arm and smiled up at her. "Thank you," I said in English.

"You are so very welcome, Tatyana," she answered, hugging me to her side with her one free arm.

I was astonished that this sweet, kind woman would treat me to a new outfit. To this day, every time I think about Mrs. Rose and her family, my heart fills with gratitude.

****

After living with the Rose family for a couple of months, it was time for us to move out on our own. Papa, Sasha and I found a small apartment filled with furnishings donated by the Assembly of God church. It was a very simple home, but we had enough to live comfortably.

There were four other Russian families living in our apartment complex, and we quickly befriended them. We had summer picnics and get-togethers, and Sasha and I played games with their children. We also found a Russian church not far from our town, and started attending service every Sunday.

One Sunday, as we were leaving church, I noticed Papa smiling at a pretty, young woman behind us.

"Good morning," he said as he held open the door for her. "It's a lovely day, isn't it?"

The woman blushed, smiling back at Papa. "Good morning," she quietly answered.

Before I knew it, Papa started spending a lot of time with this young woman. He would go out on dates with her, leaving Sasha and me behind. I understood that my father needed a friend, but Sasha and I thought it was too soon for Papa to jump into a relationship—especially after everything we'd been through. Of course, I was also a little jealous because I was no longer the center of Papa's attention. I was beginning to feel like I was no longer his priority.

And secretly, my brother and I were worried about Papa. He had suffered through an unimaginable tragedy. We were hoping he would continue to stay strong and make the right decisions for our family.

But Papa was heartbroken and lonely, and he was desperate for companionship. So, our father quickly fell in love with the young woman...and before I knew it, he had an announcement to make.

"Sasha, Tatyana," he said one morning after calling us into our tiny living room. Perched side by side on the edge of the couch, Sasha and I looked at him expectantly. "I'm getting married!"

Chapter 8

Papa's News

Sasha and I were shocked to learn that Papa was remarrying so soon, just two years after my mother's death. Of course, we were happy for him, but we were also concerned. By then, I was twelve and Sasha was fifteen—we were old enough to see that Papa was moving forward too quickly.

Papa, Sasha and I were still healing from our tragedy. That irritating grain of sand continued to scratch away at my soul, and some days the pain was absolutely unbearable. Sasha and I were concerned that Papa may not be ready for another marriage so soon, but we didn't want to upset him, so we kept our opinions to ourselves.

A few months before the wedding, Papa gave us some more joyful news. His mother and father, my dear Grandma

Veronica and Grandpa Michael, were moving to the U.S. I thought I would burst with happiness. Every time I thought about the year we lived on my grandparents' farm, it warmed my heart. They had been so caring and attentive, and I had felt so loved. I could not wait to reunite with them. The thought of their arrival gave me a sense of comfort in my uncertain world.

****

One evening, just a few days before Papa's wedding, he called us to our small living room once again. "Tatyana, Sasha," he said leaning in our bedroom door. "I need to discuss something very important with you," he said. His usually smiling face had lost its shine, and I could see stress and anxiety swimming behind his blue eyes. We obediently followed Papa down the hall, and the tension in our little apartment was so thick, I could barely walk without tripping over it. As Sasha and I reached the living room, we sat down on the couch. We watched expectantly as Papa paced back and forth across the worn carpet. After a few uncomfortable moments, Papa broke the silence.

"Come," he said with a wave of his hand, motioning us to get up. Sasha and I looked at each other with puzzled faces. "We're going to see Uncle Victor." Two of my father's brothers had moved to the U.S. shortly after we arrived, and they lived in our apartment complex.

Relieved to escape the tense apartment, Sasha and I stood up and followed Papa out the door.

Uncle Victor answered his door with a huge grin. "Tatyana, Sasha. It's so good to see you!" Our uncle greeted Sasha with a pat on the back and gave me a big hug.

"Come in, come in!"

We all sat down in the cramped living room, and Uncle Victor chatted with Sasha and me. He talked to us about school and asked how we liked living in America. After a few minutes of small talk, the room fell silent.

Sasha and I were sitting next to each other on a tattered brown couch, and Papa fidgeted nervously in a fold-out chair directly across from us. Suddenly, his face grew very serious, as if a storm cloud were passing over it.

"Tatyana, Sasha..." he said with some hesitation in his voice. "As you know, I'm getting married soon. After the wedding, I will move to another city to begin a new life."

My heart plummeted into my stomach. I had no idea where this conversation was going, but I didn't like the tone of Papa's voice. I scooted closer to Sasha and grabbed his hand.

"You know, dealing with our past and all..." Papa continued as he wringed his calloused hands. "It has been terribly hard. I want to start a new family and a new life. I want to move on."

Sasha squeezed my fingers tight with his clammy hand.

"So, I think it would be best...for all of us...if," Papa continued cautiously, "well, I think it would be best if you didn't come with me...so I've decided you'll both stay here. Tatyana, you'll move in with Grandma and Grandpa, and Sasha you can live here with your Uncle Victor." Papa just sat there staring at us, his hands now resting calmly in his lap.

I felt the delicate seams in my heart begin to rip apart. My father no longer wanted me...he was leaving us behind. I slumped onto Sasha's shoulder and sobbed uncontrollably.

"Oh, Tatyana," Papa said, as he rose and walked over to the couch. "It's going to be okay."

"NO!" I shrieked, absolutely hysterical now. "No, it's NOT going to be okay!" I leapt up from the couch and pounded Papa on the chest with my fists until he grabbed onto my hands.

"Calm down, Tatyana!" he said sternly. "Please...calm down!"

"I WILL NOT calm down!" I shouted, tears streaming down my cheeks. Papa held onto my tiny fists, and I leaned my head back and let out bone-chilling sob.

"I can't live without you, Papa!" I wailed. "I CAN'T DO IT! I'll die without you, Papa! I'll DIE!"

Papa pulled me to his chest and wrapped his arms around me. I cried for what seemed like hours. Through all of it, Papa kept trying to convince me that I would be happier living with my grandparents. The entire time, Sasha sat silently on the couch with a somber look on his face. I knew he was trying to contain his tears—he was trying to act like a man. But he was also heartbroken to hear this terrible news from our father.

Later that evening, exhausted and out of tears, I limply followed Sasha and Papa back to our apartment.

"It's going to be okay, Tatyana," Papa tried yet again. "You'll see. This will be better for you and Sasha."

I didn't even have the strength to respond. I had lost my mother. I had lost my little brother and sisters. And now I was going to lose Sasha and Papa.

Once again, I could feel my heart shattering in my chest. And this time, I was positive that nothing—no one—could ever put the pieces back together again.

Back in our apartment, I stumbled down the hallway to my bedroom, and collapsed on the bed. For the next hour, I lay there feeling absolutely lifeless. After our family's tragedy, everyone had told me that I was so blessed to be left alive. But at this moment, I felt like surviving, staying alive and enduring this pain was a punishment. And that's when it came to me.

I stood up and staggered across the hall. The house was silent, so I knew Sasha and Papa were asleep. I walked into the bathroom, closed the door and quietly turned the lock on the little brass knob. After a few minutes of rummaging through the medicine cabinet, I found my father's straight razor hidden in a brown leather pouch. I gently pulled it from its cover, and the silver blade glistened in the fluorescent bathroom light.

I held the razor just millimeters from my left wrist. I would finally destroy that irritating grain of sand and put my aching soul out of its misery. And I would join my siblings in heaven. My dear Natasha, Vera, Alonna, Misha and Julia would all be waiting for me.

As I placed the cold blade against my pale skin, a wave of fear coursed through my body. In church, I had learned that committing suicide was an unforgivable sin. The preacher said that people who took their own life went straight to hell.

"What would mother do?" I thought, the blade still resting on my trembling wrist. I still had so much anger for my mother about what she had done to my siblings and herself. I had promised myself that I would never be like her. I didn't want to look like her or act like her, and I certainly didn't want to make the choices she had made.

I felt the presence of the devil in that bathroom. "Do it!" he taunted, and the wicked whispers sent chills down my spine.

I jerked the blade away from my wrist, stabbed it back into its leather pouch and dashed out of the bathroom.

I ran back to bed, yanked the covers up to my chin and breathed an angry prayer. "God, why are you punishing my family?" I could feel the tears flowing down my cheeks, dripping onto my pillow. "What have I done to deserve this? You took my brother and my sisters. You took my mother. Why would you take my Papa from me, too? Are you really there? If you were really there, you would help me!"

What I didn't realize was that God *was* helping me. His angels were all around me, protecting me—they had stopped me from killing myself that very night.

But I could not see them. I was lost.

****

The next morning, I awoke to find Papa sitting on the edge of the bed. He brushed my hair out of my face, and whispered, "Tatyana? Are you awake?" I looked up at him through bloodshot eyes and nodded. "I'm very sorry that we have to separate," he said, "but you know I will keep in touch with you."

Although I still had so much anger for my father, so many unanswered questions, I was also concerned about him. I was starting to worry if he was in a normal state of mind. I wondered if the tragedy of losing most of his family had completely broken him and turned him into a different person. But no matter what, I still loved him dearly. After looking into his tearful eyes for a moment, I sat up and flung my arms around his neck.

"Oh, Papa, I'm going to miss you so much!" I said through tears.

"I will always love you," Papa said with a trembling voice. "Tatyana, I'm sorry things have been so...so hard for you."

I wasn't sure what to say. I just felt heartbroken and numb—like an empty shell my father was throwing away before he moved on with his new life.

A few days later, after Papa's wedding, Sasha moved in with Uncle Victor, and I moved in with Grandma and Grandpa. Uncle Victor and my grandparents were shocked by my father's choice. They did not support his decision, but they wanted to help Sasha and me. So, they agreed to take us in.

Grandma Veronica was kind to me, and she did her best to take care of her broken granddaughter. She prepared homemade meals for me every day, and she started to teach me how to cook. She always made sure I did my homework, and she encouraged me to work hard in school. Grandma and Grandpa constantly prayed; in the morning, afternoon and night. If anyone came to visit them, my grandparents would pray with them as well. I felt a sense of security with them, and I felt loved. So I tried to make the best of my situation.

But moving from a spacious farm house in Ukraine to a small apartment was a difficult transition for my grandparents. They felt like they had lost their freedom. My grandfather could no longer plant tulips and vegetables like he had on the farm, and he missed the fresh air and the feel of cool soil on his hands. He did not know what to do with himself. Because Grandpa was not happy with their new lifestyle, Grandma Veronica suffered as well. Soon, they both started to search for a piece of land to buy out in the country. They were ready to go back to the way of life they had enjoyed before: Praying to God and living off the land. That was all they knew, and it was what they loved most.

The idea of moving out to the country with them frightened me. I wanted to stay in the city, near my brother, my uncles and everyone else I knew. I wanted to be near the hustle and bustle, where I could walk to school and anywhere else I may want to go. My grandparents did not own a car—so if we moved to the countryside, I would be trapped on their farm all day, every day. Every time I thought of it, I felt like I was suffocating.

But my grandparents were tied up with their own troubles. In my mind, I was a third wheel in their family, causing them extra stress and heartache. Only two years had passed since my family's tragedy, but my relatives were already acting like it had never happened. Everyone was moving on...everyone except for me. I was standing still, rooted in my horrific past as the rest of the world whirled around me. I simply could not move on. I could not forget that fateful day. I did not understand how anyone could erase it from their memory.

Although I didn't like it, I was learning to accept that all of my other family members were going to move forward—even if I couldn't keep up with them. I was beginning to understand that people change and I shouldn't expect too much from anyone. I just had to face this cold hard truth and be grateful for the occasional kind gesture I did receive from my relatives.

Mostly, I was starting to realize that I was completely on my own. Everyone else had their own problems, and they didn't have time to mend my broken heart. So I would have to learn how to help myself. It was an incredibly painful realization. And that grain of sand continued to grind away at my tender soul.

Before I knew it, I had plummeted into an even deeper pit of depression. I would lie in my bedroom, just staring at the ceiling for hours on end. I would daydream that a nice family might kidnap me, make me their daughter and give me a better life. Sometimes, I'd imagine that a handsome young man would fall in love with me, sweep me off my feet and take me far away from here.

School was challenging for me because I was not a fast learner. In order for me to learn something, I had to write it down, repeat it over and over and continually test myself. It was grueling and stressful.

The more depressed I became, the more I ate. I gained some unwanted weight, and that made me even more miserable. One day, a boy at school called me fat. That night, I made myself throw up after dinner. I became bulimic, purging every night after I ate. I lost the extra pounds, but I still kept it up—until I learned in health class how destructive this behavior was for my body. Then, I finally stopped.

I did not know where I belonged or how to feel. I just felt…lost. Unwanted. Worthless.

I went to church, but my thoughts were not about God. I was too preoccupied with my problems…and I was distracted by boys. I kept hoping I would meet a boy who would fall in love with me.

A few Ukrainian boys at church started talking to me, and I basked in their attention. I would flirt openly with them, and every now and then a boy would smile or wink at me.

That would lift me up and give me some hope. I longed to feel loved by someone, anyone.

I started making friends at church, and word quickly spread about my tragic past. The other church members looked at me with pity, and I could feel their stares. "That poor child," they whispered. "She has a hard life ahead of her."

One day after church, a lady walked right up to me and said, "I can't imagine how hard it must be to think about the future after...you know...everything you've been through." She patted me sympathetically on the shoulder. "I mean, you'll probably never marry after living through such a horrible tragedy."

I wasn't sure how to respond. I just glared at her, shocked into silence. I did not understand how adults thought, how they came to such conclusions. My mother had suffered from a severe head trauma—but I felt like these people compared me to her, as if they thought I would have the same issues. I did not realize that my future could be determined by my past.

Even though I knew my mother's actions were most likely brought on by her brain injury, I was still furious at her for how she had torn apart our family. And I started to wonder if those grownups were right—what if I did turn out like her? The thought absolutely terrified me, and I became obsessed with comparing myself with my mother. Whenever I discovered similarities in my appearance or personality, I would go above and beyond to change it. I struggled to be the exact opposite of her. I did not want to look in the mirror and be reminded of her. I wanted nothing to do with her.

****

At this point, Uncle Victor's family had moved to another town and taken Sasha with them. My brother lived an hour away from me, and we had lost touch. I missed him terribly, and I felt alone—completely alone. All I could do was try to move on and hope for the best. I had to be strong. Once I turned thirteen, I realized that no one else was going to mend my broken heart. I decided I had to take care of myself.

Chapter 9

Not Alone

That summer, my grandparents bought a piece of land in the country and we moved into a tiny mobile home. I was absolutely devastated, and I prayed to God that I would find a new home closer to the city before the next school year began. I did not want to change schools and live so far away from everyone I knew. I was desperate for an answer. And before I knew it, God sent me one.

One Sunday a few weeks after our move, I went to church with my grandparents, and I was surprised and delighted to see a familiar face. It was my old friend Julia Stepanov. We had attended the same church in Kharkov when I lived in Ukraine, and Julia's family had recently moved to the U.S.

Julia was just six months older than me. She had timid green eyes, and her long, wavy hair was as black as night.

Because she had just moved from Ukraine, she barely spoke English. Julia was still adjusting to this new culture and the American people. She dressed modestly in Ukrainian-style clothes, so she stood out from other girls our age.

Julia and I didn't have much in common, but I didn't care. I just wanted to find a new place to live. After a few Sundays of casually chatting with her, I finally worked up the courage to ask Julia if I could move in with her. Julia talked to her family about it, and to my surprise, they said yes.

Although I had prayed for an opportunity like this, I felt torn about leaving my grandparents behind. As I wrestled with my decision, I spent nights thrashing about, overcome with anxiety and horrible nightmares. I was absolutely terrified of leaving my Grandma and Grandpa, the only hint of family I had left. But I knew I could not spend one more day living in their tiny mobile home out in the country. This was the only way. As the summer came to a close, I decided to tell Grandma and Grandpa I wanted to move in with Julia's family. They were sad, but they gave me their blessing. They both understood why I wanted to stay in the city. It was the most difficult decision I'd ever made. But it ended up being the best.

Julia, her parents and her three brothers lived in the city, in the same apartment complex where Papa, Sasha and I used to live. I was so excited and grateful that they had opened up their home to me. My father paid Mr. and Mrs. Stepanov for all of my living expenses. I went to church with the Stepanov family every Sunday, and Julia and I were registered to attend the same school in the fall.

But when I first moved in with Julia, it felt awkward because we were so different. In fact, we were polar opposites. Not only did we look and dress differently, but we also had completely different personalities. She was quiet and shy and always kept to herself. I was more outgoing, often speaking too soon and saying things I did not mean. Although Julia rarely talked to boys, I was overly flirtatious. I craved attention and was constantly trying to gain love and affection from the boys at church.

"You are a flirtatious girl," Julia told me one day. "You are a flirt, and you need God in your life." I was surprised at her brutal honesty, but I did not care. At least I thought I didn't care. I tried to act tough—but deep inside that grain of sand was silently scratching away at my wounded soul.

Julia was incredibly calm. Although she came across as bashful, she was full of confidence and self-control. She tried not worry about what anyone else thought about her. I, on the other hand, did not care about life that much. I tried not to dwell on my past or imagine my future. The future scared me. So, I did not think about much of anything. I just lived day by day, moment by moment.

I was not aggressive, but I was certainly rebellious. I had a few favorite curse words that I learned in middle school, and I liked to toss them around, hoping to shock my friends.

One day, I decided to try smoking. After I stole a cigarette from one of my uncles, I snuck into the alley behind our complex. But when I pulled the cigarette out of my pocket, I realized it had broken in half. I let out a stream of curses, threw the ruined cigarette to the ground and stormed back to Julia's apartment.

Life had become so uncertain for me. I was tired of feeling pain, so I just tried to make myself numb to everything. I was not bitter or angry or passionate...I was simply existing.

Julia and I shared a tiny bedroom. We did not have much privacy, so we just learned how to deal with each other. I was glad to have a place to live, and she was glad to have a friend—at least, she hoped we would be close friends one day.

I watched Julia pray every night. She had amazing willpower and stability—qualities I knew I lacked. Although we were the same age, Julia acted so much more mature than me. At first I thought she was boring. But something about her drew me in, and I decided I liked her. Before I knew it, I started to feel incredibly comfortable with her. It was as if I had gained a sister.

One evening, Julia and I were hanging out in our quiet bedroom. I was sprawled on the floor flipping through the pages of a magazine and Julia was sitting on her bed doing homework. Suddenly, Julia broke the silence. "What do you want to be when you grow up?"

Startled by her voice, I glanced up and saw her staring at me with those intense green eyes. "Umm...I don't know," I said looking back down at my magazine. I slowly flipped the page. "I haven't really thought about it."

"Oh," she said, sounding a little disappointed. "Well, do you plan on getting married? Do you want to have kids?"

I suddenly heard an echo of Natasha's sweet voice from a few years before: *I want a wedding dress just like the one mother wore.* But I quickly crushed the memory before it had time to blossom into sadness.

"I don't know," I said, still turning the pages of my magazine. I was trying not to look up at Julia.

"So, you don't think about the future at all?" she asked. "You don't have any hopes or dreams?"

I kept staring at my magazine, pretending to be fascinated with an article about makeup trends for the season. But the printed words began to swirl as tears welled up in my eyes.

"Yes, I have dreams, okay? But they'll never come true," I said, keeping my eyes glued to my magazine.

Julia climbed down from her bed and sat next to me on the carpet. "Why do you think that?" she asked. I could feel her heavy gaze on me. I slapped the magazine shut, sat up and looked her straight in the eye.

"Because of my...my past," I answered. Julia knew about my family's tragedy, but we didn't talk about it often.

"People are always telling me that things will be really hard for me," I continued. "Everyone feels sorry for me. They all seem to think my life will be awful. And I guess they're probably right."

But deep in my heart, I still didn't understand why people thought this way. My mother had suffered from a terrible head trauma, and no one had understood the seriousness of her condition—until it was too late. My family members made a horrible mistake by not getting her the help she needed. But I just couldn't understand what all this had to do with *my* life. Why was my life doomed just because all of that had happened?

I had heard the old saying that the apple does not fall far from the tree. Maybe people assumed I would be just like my mother. I figured that's what they meant when they said my life would be hard and I would never marry. Even if I was healthy and normal, who in the world would take a chance and marry me after what my mother had done? So yes, I had dreams...but I did not think any of them would come true.

I tried to explain all of this to Julia. She remained silent for a long time, just staring at the floor. I could tell she was deep in thought about something.

Then suddenly, she looked up at me with those determined emerald eyes and asked me a life-changing question. "Tatyana, are you happy with yourself?"

I just sat as still as a stone, allowing that question to soak into my soul. My heart started racing, and all that pain I had pushed down deep inside started to bubble up to the surface.

"Please don't be mad at me for asking you," she said, and I could sense the reluctance in her voice. "But I want to know...are you truly happy with yourself? Are you happy with who you are? Are you happy with the way you act?"

I wanted to give her a response...but I did not have the answer. "I—I don't know," I said with a trembling voice. "I'll have to think about it."

She just nodded, her long, raven ponytail bouncing on her head. And that was the end of our conversation. We both quietly worked on our homework, and we barely spoke for the rest of the evening.

"Are you mad at me?" Julia would ask every so often.

"No," I'd answer quietly, keeping my eyes glued to my notebook.

But deep down, I was troubled.

****

For the next few days, I pondered Julia's question. I kept hearing her voice in my head, repeating over and over, "Tatyana, are you happy with yourself?"

I couldn't pinpoint it, but there was something missing. I felt as if there were a gaping hole inside of me. I had very low expectations for myself. I never dreamed about my future or a career. I was not spiritual. All I wanted was love, and I spent my days trying to seek out attention and affection—especially from boys.

I was beginning to realize that I was *not* happy with myself. When I looked in the mirror, I hated what I saw. I wanted to borrow some of Julia's qualities. I wanted to be more confident, more stable. I wanted to be calmer, gentler, kinder. I wanted to stop worrying about what other people thought about me. I wanted boys to be attracted to me because they liked who I was—not because I threw myself at them. I wanted to be loved. I wanted to love *myself*.

I realized there had to be more to me. There must be some greater purpose in my life. There must be some reason why I had survived such a horrific tragedy.

A few days later, I walked into our bedroom and closed the door behind me. "No," I said to Julia, who was perched on the bed with an American History book in her lap.

"Huh?" she said, looking up at me with a puzzled expression.

"The answer is no," I said, setting my backpack on the floor. "No, I am not happy with myself."

It was extremely difficult for me to utter those words out loud. It was an enormous act of humility. But as soon as it escaped my mouth, I felt relieved. I could already feel a change happening inside of me. I felt like my soul was thawing, the numbness slowly fading.

Julia stared at me for a few moments. Then, she stood up from the bed, walked over and hugged me. I burst into tears. It was the first time I'd allowed myself to cry since Papa had left.

"Can you help me?" I sniffled, burying my face in her jet-black curls. "Can you tell me how to be a better person?"

"Of course," she said. "I'm just so glad you're not mad at me!"

We both broke out into giggles and collapsed onto the bed. I wiped at my eyes and smiled at her. My heart swelled with love for Julia...my best friend. My sister.

****

So Julia shared her secrets with me. She broke it down for me and explained what truly believing in Jesus means. She told me that Jesus died for me and rose again for me. She promised that if I were to accept Jesus Christ into my heart, every part of me would change. She said I would think differently, speak differently, feel differently and act differently.

"But you have to pray all the time," she said. "God is always listening...you just have to talk to him."

I knew deep in my heart that if I refused to follow God, my life would be yet another tragedy. I was already battling depression and thoughts of suicide. God was my only way out of this mess.

I was so exhausted of searching for happiness, and I realized that I couldn't measure my worth by how much I was loved by other people. I wanted to love myself...and most importantly, I wanted to understand the full measure of my Heavenly Father's love for me.

So I decided to take Julia's advice and keep believing in God and His Word. There was a part of me that wanted to see if God could really help me. One quiet night, as I was listening to soft worship music alone in our bedroom, I knelt down on quivering knees, closed my eyes and prayed to God earnestly. "God please help me to be more like Jesus,"

I prayed. "I want to be complete. I don't want to depend on anyone else, and I don't want to be alone."

And then, I felt the hot tears streaming down my cheeks. I wept freely before God. I told Him everything. I told Him how I did not truly understand all the terrible things that had happened to me—all the tragedies I had faced throughout my short life. But that night I promised Him that despite my unanswered questions about my horrific past, and no matter what the future may bring, I would praise and honor Him with my life.

As I whispered my prayer through quiet sobs, I felt His presence fill the tiny bedroom—and an overwhelming sense of peace and hope flooded my heart and rushed into my soul. As I continued to pray, I heard my favorite song playing in the background: "*You are my hiding place, You always fill my heart with songs of deliverance whenever I am afraid…I will trust in You.*"

That night, after I felt the Lord's warming presence in my room, I chose to put all of my trust in Jesus from that day forward. I repeated my favorite Psalm over and over again: "*The Lord is my shepherd, I shall not be in want. He makes me lie down in green pastures, he leads me beside quiet waters, he restores my soul. He guides me in paths of righteousness for his name's sake. Even though I walk through the valley of the shadow of death, I will fear no evil, for you are with me; your rod and your staff, they comfort me. You prepare a table before me in the presence of my enemies. You anoint my head with oil; my cup overflows. Surely good-ness and love will follow me all the days of my life, and I will dwell in the house of the Lord forever." (Psalm 23)*

I vowed to pray as often as possible, to read the Bible, and most importantly, to do as the Bible said. Julia and I began to attend Bible studies in our church together. I also confessed all of my sins to one of the church elders, and I accepted freedom from my sins and any generational curses through Jesus Christ. I felt such an enormous relief after I confessed my sins out loud and accepted victory through Jesus Christ.

The church elders explained in detail what Jesus did on the cross for me, and they read Romans 5:6-11 to me: *"You see, at just the right time, when we were still powerless, Christ died for the ungodly. Very rarely will anyone die for a righteous man, though for a good man someone might possibly dare to die. But God demonstrates his own love for us in this: While we were still sinners, Christ died for us. Since we have now been justified by his blood, how much more shall we be saved from God's wrath through him! For if, when we were God's enemies, we were reconciled to him through the death of his Son, how much more, having been reconciled, shall we be saved through his life! Not only is this so, but we also rejoice in God through our Lord Jesus Christ, through whom we have now received reconciliation."*

I believed that Jesus died for me so I could have a brand new life, and I understood that I could not live a selfish and sinful life. I read in the book of Romans where the Apostle Paul explains how God has provided for our redemption and justification:

"Or don't you know that all of us who were baptized into Christ Jesus were baptized into his death? We were therefore buried with him through baptism into death in order that, just as Christ was raised from the dead through the glory of the Father, we too may live a new life.

If we have been united with him like this in his death, we will certainly also be united with him in his resurrection. For we know that our old self was crucified with him so that the body of sin might be done away with, that we should no longer be slaves to sin—because anyone who has died has been freed from sin.

Now if we died with Christ, we believe that we will also live with him. For we know that since Christ was raised from the dead, he cannot die again; death no longer has mastery over him. The death he died, he died to sin once for all; but the life he lives, he lives to God.

In the same way, count yourselves dead to sin but alive to God in Christ Jesus. Therefore do not let sin reign in your mortal body so that you obey its evil desires. Do not offer the parts of your body to sin, as instruments of wickedness, but rather offer yourselves to God, as those who have been brought from death to life; and offer the parts of your body to him as instruments of righteousness. For sin shall not be your master, because you are not under law, but under grace." (Romans 6:3-14)

I started to observe and learn from other people's mistakes, and I read more about sin in the Bible. I realized that sin always leads to bad consequences. I also understood that when someone sins, their transgressions do not just affect them, but also everyone close to them. As Romans 6:16 says, *"Don't you know that when you offer yourselves to someone to obey him as slaves, you are slaves to the one whom you obey—whether you are slaves to sin, which leads to death, or to obedience, which leads to righteousness?"*

The more I read, the more I began to understand the Bible in a very personal way. It was as if I had experienced a new revelation about everything I had believed all of my life—however, I suddenly connected with those beliefs on a much more profound level. I deeply understood that faith is about accepting Jesus, and I made a serious decision to follow Him. I truly believed in the verse from the book of Isaiah: *"But he was pierced for our transgressions, he was crushed for our iniquities; the punishment that brought us*

peace was upon him, and by his wounds we are healed."
(Isaiah 53:5)

As soon as I believed in what Jesus did for me, I could feel *my* wounds starting to heal. I had a newfound hope for the future, and I realized my future would have nothing to do with my past. I believed that there was victory in the name of Jesus. I realized how helpless I was without God. I couldn't rely on my own strength—what gave me strength was what Jesus did on the cross for me so I could overcome all my fears, depression and loneliness. I believed that He would direct my decisions and protect me.

I continued to turn to one particular Bible verse from the book of Proverbs, a verse that still leaves me speechless every time I read it today: *"Trust in the Lord with all your heart and lean not on your own understanding; in all your ways acknowledge him, and he will make your paths straight." (Proverbs 3:5-6)* I was learning how to remain in God's presence no matter where I went, and I finally understood how to surrender my life to God and trust in Him—and it was such a relief. I was beginning to let go and show humility before God.

I also grew very sensitive to the Holy Spirit, and I started to sense what was good for me and what would not be beneficial in my life. As my fourteenth birthday quickly approached, I was slowly maturing, becoming a more beautiful young lady, transforming from the inside out. I also discovered self-control. I embraced the verse from Proverbs that says, *"Like a city whose walls are broken down is a man who lacks self-control."* *(Proverbs 25:28)* I did not want to be like that city, unprotected and vulnerable to the enemies. As Titus 2:11-12 says, *"For the grace of God that brings salvation has appeared to all men. It teaches us to say "No" to ungodliness and worldly passions, and to live self-controlled, upright and godly lives."*

My life was not all about me anymore—it was about doing God's will. I genuinely wanted to please God, so I strived to follow the Word of God to the best of my ability. I knew that I could not do it on my own, so I prayed to Jesus to help me every day. I literally lived an hour at a time. I stopped worrying about the future, and I lived in each moment with Jesus.

I often turned to the teaching that Jesus told His disciples in the book of Matthew. He said, *"Therefore I tell you, do not worry about your life, what you will eat or drink; or about your body, what you will wear. Is not life more important than food, and the body more important than clothes? Look at the birds of the air; they do not sow or reap or store away in barns, and yet your heavenly Father feeds them. Are you not much more valuable than they? Who of you by worrying can add a single hour to his life?"* *(Matthew 6:25-27)*

As I read that Bible verse, I looked back on those dark times when people had told me I would probably never get married because of my tragic past. But, after becoming a follower of Christ, I stopped worrying about the future or fretting over whether or not I would get married. In fact, I decided that if I never got married, it would be fine—that I would simply dedicate my life to serving God. At one point, I even considered being a nun. I truly wanted to serve others and fulfill the will of God for my life.

I was not worried anymore. And if I did feel worry creeping into my heart, I turned to the Word of God. When I read the Bible, it always put me back on the right path and helped me regain focus on my purpose: To follow Christ and fulfill His will in my life. I decided to build my life on the Word of God. The Word of God served as my map, leading me in the right direction.

That summer, at the young age of fourteen, I decided to receive water baptism. I knew that if Jesus was baptized in the water, I had to follow His example. Julia decided to get baptized as well, and we joined a water baptism class together. We learned that Jesus commanded all His followers to receive water baptism. "*Then Jesus came to them and said, 'All authority in heaven and on earth has been given to me. Therefore go and make disciples of all nations, baptizing them in the name of the Father and of the Son and of the Holy Spirit, and teaching them to obey everything I have commanded you. And surely I am with you always, to the very end of the age.'" (Matthew 28:18-20)*

Julia and I spent a few weeks preparing for the baptism, and before we knew it, the day had arrived. Our pastor had chosen a small lake for the baptism ceremony. It was a warm summer day, the brilliant sun glistening in a cloudless sky overhead, reflecting on the surface of the glassy lake. Julia and I and the rest of our classmates from the baptism class were dressed all in white, and our entire church congregation gathered on the bank of the lake. I looked out in the crowd and spotted Papa and his new family standing to witness my baptism. By now, Papa and his wife had a beautiful baby girl. I also caught a glimpse of my dear brother, Sasha. I felt my face burst into a smile as I waved excitedly to them.

The praise and worship group lifted their voices up in sweet song, and the pastor began to baptize us, dipping us one by one in the cool green lake water. When it was my turn, the pastor asked me to make my confession out loud before all the people. I announced proudly, "Jesus is my Lord and my Savior." Then the pastor said, "I baptize you in the name of the Father, Son and the Holy Spirit." As he lowered me into the sun-streaked water, I looked up into the clear blue sky and whispered a quick prayer to God: "I will follow you all of the days of my life." The pastor dipped me briefly beneath the gleaming surface, and my world momentarily went silent. As he lifted me back up, I heard the water rushing against my ears, and I emerged feeling like I had been reborn.

Although I did not experience anything supernatural that day or hear the Lord speak to me, I knew what the baptism signified: I was reborn to a new life with God. He had created me in His image, and through Him I had discovered a life of victory. I was excited to begin a new journey with Christ, and I believed with all of my heart that through Jesus I was a new person.

After the baptism, Papa raced up to me, a bouquet of beautiful flowers clenched in his hand. "I am so proud of you, Tatyana," he said, wrapping his strong arms around my wet shoulders.

"Papa," I giggled. "You'll get all wet!"

"Oh, I don't mind," he said with a laugh as he pulled away and handed me the flowers.

My brother Sasha gave me the best gift of all that day: my own personal Bible. He had written a verse from the Bible on the inside of the cover as a dedication to me: "*I love those who love me, and those who seek me find me.*" (*Proverbs 8:17*)

Later that day, I decided to dedicate a verse from the Bible to myself, and I carefully wrote it under my brother's verse: *"Be faithful, even to the point of death, and I will give you the crown of life." (Revelation 2:10)* I knew that serving Jesus may not always be easy, but I was ready for my journey to begin with Him carrying me through it all. To this day, I still have that precious Bible, with the two hand-written verses in the front.

Later that day, after the baptism, I participated in communion for the first time in my life, and it was an amazing experience. I truly felt like I was starting my life over again, and I couldn't wait to see where this new life would take me.

After the communion, I hugged Sasha goodbye and thanked him for the Bible. By this time, Sasha had graduated from high school and was attending a university in another city, but we always tried to keep in touch. We didn't talk as often as I would have liked, but we knew that we loved each other. Papa and I also kept in touch. Although Papa's decision had separated us, I still loved my family very much.

Whenever Papa and I saw each other, he would tell me, "My dear daughter, never, ever give up. And remember Tatyana—God is always watching you. "His words always reminded me that Christianity is all about what you do when no one is watching but God Himself.

Although we had been through a lot of turmoil together, I did not hate my father. I had a very forgiving heart, especially once I started learning more about the Bible. I was actually much more concerned about my father than myself. I realized that he had suffered through a lot of pain himself, and I always prayed that God would heal his heart and help him be the best father and husband for his new family.

One verse in the Bible always helped me realize that we live in a very spiritual world, and the type of spirit that lives in each person will determine the decisions that person makes: *"For our struggle is not against flesh and blood, but against the rulers, against the authorities, against the powers of this dark world and against the spiritual forces of evil in the heavenly realms." (Ephesians 6:12)* If the Spirit of God lives in a person, then that person will be blessed with the fruits of the Spirit: love, joy, peace, forbearance, kindness, goodness, faithfulness, gentleness and self-control. This verse from Ephesians helped me understand that my battle is not against any person. Like never before, I wanted to make sure that I always had the spirit of God in me. I knew that I needed to follow Jesus and stay safely under His protection to make it in this life.

I was learning how to remain in God's presence no matter where I went. I finally understood how to surrender my life to God and trust in Him, and it was such a relief. He was the single pair of footprints in the sand, carrying me through my most difficult times. But I had not truly given myself over to Him until now. I once was lost, and now I was found. And I felt joy blooming inside of me.

I had surrendered all and dedicated my life to God. Thus, a new chapter in my life began.

Chapter 10

A New Life

I was astounded by the miracles that started to happen in my life. My depression quickly melted away, and I did not long for attention as I had before. I was overcome with humility and felt a seed of confidence sprouting deep in my soul.

I was seeking God with all my heart and mind. Deep inside my heart, I knew I was finally on the right path. I just had to keep moving in that direction. I suddenly began to feel so much love for the people around me. I started to notice people who needed reassurance. I would reach out to them with a word of encouragement, and Christ's love would flow through me and into their lives. I was so excited to serve others and inspire them by sharing the gospel of Jesus Christ.

I barely recognized myself. I was becoming so unselfish, and I finally understood that I had to serve others just like Jesus did. It made me so much happier to give love instead of simply receiving it. Anyway, I received plenty of love from God. Each day, He showed me His love in a new way.

I was suddenly grateful for ordinary, everyday things. It did not take much to please me. I did not have much, but what I had was enough. God had blessed me with a happy home at Julia's house and a nice group of friends in church. I learned to live with little but to always be grateful for what I had.

I constantly listened to worship music. Those healing melodies drifted into my injured soul, bringing peace to my heart.

Soon, the jagged grain of sand that had been scraping away at my soul for all those years started to soften. I could feel God's love slowly wrapping around it, layer upon layer, protecting my tender soul from the pain. And before I knew it, that tragic grain had transformed into something truly miraculous and beautiful: a tiny pearl of hope.

****

My freshman year of high school flew by. I realized if I studied hard enough, I could actually make A's. When it came time for exams, I would study very hard and pray the night before the test. By the grace of God, this method always worked well, and I continued to make good grades. Unlike middle school, our high school was very big. There were plenty of bullies and lots of peer pressure, but I found a way to ignore all the distractions. I kept my head up to Jesus, minded my own business and worked hard.

On the last day of our freshman year, Julia and I walked to school together. It was a warm June morning, and the sweet smell of honeysuckle lingered in the air. I glanced over at Julia and noticed how the sunlight danced in her shiny, dark hair. As I looked at her, I felt overcome with gratitude. I silently thanked God for bringing her into my life.

Julia caught me looking at her and smiled at me. "You have changed, Tatyana," she said. "It's like you are a completely different person."

I just grinned and nodded. She giggled and grabbed a hold of my fingers. As we strolled down the sidewalk together hand in hand, I thought of the days when Natasha and I walked to school together in Ukraine. I turned my face up to the apricot sun glowing in a cloudless sky, and I suddenly felt my twin sister smiling down on me. And I knew she was proud of who I had become.

****

The next fall, Julia and I started our sophomore year. We both studied hard and excelled in school. But more than anything, we enjoyed attending our church youth group.

That year, a new boy joined the youth group. His name was Paul, and from the moment I laid eyes on him, I knew he was different. He had sandy blonde hair and the kindest hazel-blue eyes. He was very handsome, and he had this amazing energy that drew people to him. Although Paul went to a different high school, I had heard about him.

Not only was Paul a great athlete, but he was also a talented musician. He sang, acted and played violin. Everyone seemed to know him, and all the youth members admired his musical talents.

"Hi there," he said to me one day as we were walking out of the youth group meeting. "I don't think we've met. My name is Paul."

"Hi," I answered shyly, glancing up at his friendly blue eyes. "I know who you are. I'm pretty sure everyone does!" I giggled. "I'm Tatyana."

From that day on, Paul and I talked after every youth meeting. We had very similar beliefs about life, and we were both devoted Christians. Over the next two years, we became inseparable friends. Paul was incredibly smart and attentive, and I thought he was the sweetest guy in the world.

One night, a couple of years after Paul and I first met, we were at a friend's birthday party. As we all gathered around the candle-lit cake and sang "Happy Birthday," I realized

Paul was not standing with us. I glanced around the room and spotted him sulking in a corner. He had not been himself for a few days, and I could tell something was troubling him.

After our friend blew out her candles, I tapped Julia on the shoulder and whispered, "I'll be right back." I walked over to where Paul was standing.

"Hey, do you want to talk?" I asked.

"Umm, yeah," he said, glancing up at me before anxiously turning his gaze back to the floor. "Yes, I would love to talk. Why don't we walk outside?"

"Okay," I replied. He turned and shoved his hands in his pockets as he strolled toward the door. I followed him, a strange mix of hope and fear bubbling up inside of me.

As we walked out of our friend's apartment, the chilly air sent a shiver down my spine. It was a perfectly clear winter night in upstate New York, with not even a wisp of a cloud in the sky. Paul and I walked in silence through the apartment parking lot. We eventually ran into a flight of huge pavement steps that wound up a steep hill before disappearing into the darkness. "Let's go up there," Paul said, tilting his head toward the steps.

We climbed the steps, side by side, until we made it to the top. As Paul and I reached the highest peak of the hill, I couldn't believe my eyes. Stretched out below us was the entire city, a sea of twinkling lights that reached all the way to the distant horizon. It took my breath away. As we stood there in the grass admiring the city below, I looked up at the navy blue canopy overhead and saw an endless vista of stars winking down at us.

"Wow," I whispered, craning my neck up to the sky. "What a beautiful sight."

"Yes, it is," Paul answered quietly. When I looked back at him, I saw that he was not gazing at the stars or the view of the city—he was looking directly at me.

Suddenly, he took a couple of steps closer and leaned into my face. I could feel his lips brush against my ear as he whispered, "Tatyana...I like you more than a friend."

Startled by the warmth of his breath on my cold ear, I stepped back. "What do you mean...more than a friend?"

"Tatyana," he said, stuffing his hands back into his pockets. "I...well...I guess I'm trying to say..." He nervously shuffled his feet in the grass and looked out at the sparkling city below. "I'm trying to say that I love you. And I want to spend the rest of my life with you."

I was shocked by his words—but at the same moment, I felt so loved. I felt warmth surge through my soul, and I knew in my heart that I was meant to spend the rest of my life with Paul. We were young, but I was absolutely certain Paul was the one for me.

I smiled at him for a few seconds, feeling the flush rise to my cheeks. Finally I said, "I feel the same way about you." He beamed at me, and I saw relief wash over his face.

"But...there are some things I need to tell you," I said.

Later that night, as Paul drove me home, I told him my life story. I wanted him to be aware of my past. I was completely honest with him.

I did not spare him any detail. I told him about my mother's head injury. I told him about my siblings and the terrible tragedy. I told him about moving to America and my father's decision to remarry and leave Sasha and me behind. I told him about my depression and my near-attempt at suicide. I told him about when I truly found God.

He sat quietly, focusing on the road, listening to every word. Every now and then, I thought I saw tears glisten in his hazel eyes. A couple of times, he grabbed my hand and squeezed my fingers, as if he wanted to comfort me and take away the pain.

When I finally finished, he said, "I'm so, so sorry, Tatyana. I'm sorry for...everything you've been through. And, I still love you. I will *always* love you."

I was overcome with joy. Despite my tragic past, Paul still loved me. I had never felt so loved in all my life.

That night, we made a promise to each other that we would marry soon. We were only seventeen years old.

****

Later that spring, Paul invited me to his high school prom. He showed me off as if I were the most beautiful girl in the world. He made me feel more special and important than I had felt in a very long time. We both graduated from high school that year.

After high school, Paul was accepted into music school, but the tuition was too expensive. His family could not afford it, so he had to turn down the opportunity. I was heartbroken for him, but he didn't seem too upset. I think he was more focused on starting our life together.

At the time, I was working as a waitress at a local restaurant. One evening, soon after I graduated from high school, I stumbled into my apartment, exhausted after a long day of work. I was just starting to change out of my uniform when the phone rang.

I sighed and picked up the receiver with a sleepy, "Hello?" As soon as I heard Paul's voice on the line, I felt wide awake. We'd been together for almost a year, but my heart still skipped a beat whenever I heard his soothing voice or saw his handsome face.

"Hey there," he said. "I'd like to spend some time with you tonight. I want to…talk to you about something. Are you free?"

"Yes, of course!" I answered with grin. "Why don't you pick me up in about an hour?"

By the time I climbed into Paul's car that night, it was completely dark outside, and a full moon was shining down on us. Paul drove around looking for the perfect spot to stop and talk, but all the local restaurants were closed.

"Well, I guess it's too late to grab a bite to eat," he said with a secretive little smile. I smiled back at him, wondering what was on his mind.

The next thing I knew, he pulled into the parking lot of a little white wooden church. He opened my car door, took my hand and led me around the side of the old church. As we were walking, a flash of light on the ground caught my eye. I looked down and saw that about five feet ahead of us, there was a sparkling object hidden in the grass. "What on Earth is that?" Paul asked as he led me to it.

When we reached the spot, I bent down and saw a small gift box wrapped in glittery silver paper with a sparkly ribbon tied on top. I looked back up at Paul, who was standing over me.

"Well…aren't you going to open it?" he said with a huge smile on his handsome face.

I suddenly realized what was happening, and I felt excitement course through my veins. I stood up and tore the ribbon and paper from the package. Inside, there was a tiny red velvet box. I slowly opened it and found tucked in the box's shiny white satin, a simple but beautiful diamond ring. I gasped, and before I knew it Paul was down on one knee in front of me.

"Tatyana," he said. "I know I've asked you once before, but I wanted to make it official. Will you marry me?"

"YES, of course I will!" I laughed. He carefully slipped the ring on my finger, and I leapt into his arms. I had never felt happier in my entire life. At only eighteen years old, I had found my soul mate. I was truly in heaven.

****

Soon after Paul proposed, we started to plan our wedding—but we faced many obstacles. Some of Paul's family members did not want him to marry me. Of course, I understood why. Everyone wants their child to marry someone with a fairly normal background. And my past was anything but normal.

"Paul, if you have any doubts in your heart, you don't have to marry me," I told him. "It's okay…I just want you to be happy."

"No, Tatyana," Paul answered in a serious voice. "You are the only one for me. We *will* get married."

Fortunately, Paul's parents supported our relationship. They realized their son was truly in love with me. We knew that some other people were not happy for us, but it didn't matter. We were so deeply in love, and we spent every free moment together. Every time I saw Paul walk into a room, my heart inflated like a balloon.

The big day finally arrived. The day of our wedding, I got ready by myself. My friend Julia was already married with a baby, and she did not have time to serve as a bridesmaid. So that morning, I went to the hair salon by myself and dressed in my wedding gown alone.

Today, it brings tears to my eyes knowing that I could not share those special moments with a dear friend—or a sister. But at the time, I did not think twice about the loneliness of it all. I knew God was with me on that special day, and I could not wait to marry my best friend.

My dear Aunt Olga, Uncle Victor's wife, sewed my wedding gown for me. One of my friends gave me her old wedding dress, and my sweet aunt somehow found the time to turn it into the perfect dress for me. Although she had five children to take care of, Aunt Olga spent many sleepless nights slaving over that gown. She lovingly crafted flowers with her own two hands and sewed them to the dress. It was an absolutely stunning gown, and I was so grateful.

When Paul picked me up to drive me to the church, I was already wearing the wedding dress.

"Wow," he said as he stood, awe-struck, at my front door. "Tatyana, you look absolutely beautiful."

I beamed as he opened the car door for me. I could not believe this was happening to me. As we drove to the church, it seemed like a dream. Paul and I were so young and inexperienced, but it didn't matter. All we knew was that we loved each other more than anything—and that we wanted to devote our lives to God.

When I arrived at the church, Papa was waiting for me. "Oh, Tatyana," he said, as he rushed to my side. "You look lovely. I am so happy for you." He squeezed my hand and kissed me gently on the cheek, and I could see tears glistening in his eyes.

"Thank you, Papa," I said with a smile.

He wiped at his eyes and said, "Okay. Are you ready?"

I nodded. Papa took my arm, and the next thing I knew, the doors to the church burst open. As Papa and I walked down the aisle together, we gazed out at a sea of smiling faces, all of our dear friends and family looking back at us. And then I looked down the aisle and saw Paul waiting in front of the pulpit, his loving eyes gleaming with happiness. My heart leapt with joy.

During the wedding ceremony, Paul and I took turns praying, thanking God for blessing us with each other. We publicly dedicated our lives to God and asked Him to protect us on the journey we were about to begin. Papa and Paul's mother and father also prayed for our marriage, and we received their kind blessings. After we exchanged rings and shared a tender kiss, we were officially husband and wife. Paul and I beamed with joy as we walked back down the aisle hand in hand. And then we headed to the reception to celebrate our special day.

We did not have much money for the wedding, so our families helped out as much as they could. We rented out a building, and our parents and their friends catered the reception. Each person brought a delicious homemade dish, and there was tons of food.

The reception area was decorated in peach—all the place settings, flowers and decorations were the same soothing shade. It felt so warm and earthy. A band from our church played music. It was simple, but beautiful and pure.

During the reception, Paul shocked everyone when he dedicated a wedding song to me. "This is the day that the Lord hath made, and I will rejoice he made YOU," he sang in his gorgeous voice. It was absolutely beautiful, and everyone was surprised—especially me.

I kept thinking to myself, "My best friend is now my husband—and I am his wife."

****

After the wedding, we moved into a little house that Paul's parents rented out to us.

"Call us Mom and Dad," his parents would tell me. At first, it was difficult to get used to calling them that. But in time, it became natural for me.

As soon as we married, Paul and I went out to search for jobs. I worked as a bank teller, and Paul delivered pizzas. We quickly realized that we needed to go to college and earn degrees.

A few months later, I heard about a dental hygiene program in our area. Paul and I both wanted to have children, and I thought working as a dental hygienist would be a great career for a mom.

When I joined the school, I had no idea it would be one of the toughest challenges I would ever face. The program included tons of information condensed into just three years, and it was incredibly intense. Some of the girls in my class literally suffered from nervous breakdowns.

One day, I came home from class to find Paul in our tiny kitchen. "I can't do it," I said, slamming my books on the counter. "This program is just too hard…it's unbearable. I'm ready to quit."

Paul wrapped his arms around me, and held me tight. "I want you to be happy, Tatyana. If dropping out of the program will make you happy, then go ahead," he whispered. "But I know you can do this, Tatyana. I know you can."

But I still had my doubts. Fortunately, there was a Ukrainian girl named Lena in the program with me. She had only lived in the U.S. for two years. When I told her I was thinking about leaving the program, she stared at me for what felt like an eternity.

"Tatyana," she finally said, "If I am not giving up, then why are you?" Suddenly, my father's words echoed in my mind: *"Tatyana, never give up. Remember, God is always watching you."*

I thought long and hard about what Lena said, and I realized I had no good reason to give up. The program was extremely challenging, but I had overcome much tougher challenges before. So I decided to give it my all.

I prayed constantly because I knew without God's help I would never pass. "God, please help me get through this program," I would pray, "and I promise to give you all the glory and honor."

I may not have been the smartest person in my class, but I was a very hard worker with a willing heart and a strong desire to learn. One of my teachers, Mrs. Miller, saw this in me. She would encourage me and offer me extra help whenever I needed it. Every time I started to doubt myself, Mrs. Miller would say, "Tatyana, you are doing wonderfully. You are a natural."

One day in clinical training, I was lying in the dental chair and Mrs. Miller was standing over me discussing how to search for cavities. Suddenly, she went silent, and I noticed she was staring down at me with a strange look on her face.

"Tatyana," she whispered. "What are those scars on your neck?"

I felt a flash of pain, and nervous heat rushed through my body. My eyes started to fill with tears, but I pushed them back. I wanted so badly to tell Mrs. Miller the truth so she could truly know me. I wanted her to understand me and feel my pain. But I did not tell her the full story.

I pulled myself together, and quickly answered, "It was...a tragedy." This was always how I answered when people asked me about my scars or my past. I simply told them it was a tragedy. Just a tragedy. I did not want them to know the details of my terrible secret.

I saw a look of pity flash across Mrs. Miller's face. She quickly replaced it with a warm smile before continuing with her class.

Mrs. Miller never asked me about my past again— but she continued to encourage and help me whenever I needed it. And for that, I am eternally grateful.

Three long years after I started the dental hygiene program, I graduated with honors. I could not believe it. I had finally realized that with hard work and God by my side, nothing was impossible. I felt extremely proud.

Toward the end of the dental hygiene program, I learned that I was pregnant. Paul and I were ecstatic. We could not wait to welcome a sweet child into our lives. But soon after we were blessed with the pregnancy, I had a miscarriage.

I was absolutely heartbroken, and I struggled to survive the storm. I started to wonder how many more tragedies I would have to face in my lifetime. I feared that I may never have children. The thought made me feel hollow, like my womb was an endless abyss of sadness.

But I decided to humble myself before God once again. I knew there must be some reason for this misfortune— something I simply could not understand. I made a decision to add it to the list of unanswered questions I will one day put before Him.

And thanks be to God, soon after I graduated, I learned I was pregnant again. Nine months later, I gave birth to a beautiful, healthy baby boy. Paul and I named him Matthew. Our sweet Matthew grew up into a brilliant little boy, so smart and confident.

Three and a half years later I gave birth to our second son, Mark. From the day he was born, Mark was a tough little guy—intelligent, yet energetic and fearless.

Mark wants to be a doctor when he grows up, and Matthew wants to be an inventor and scientist. They both bring me so much love and joy. I love them so completely, so dearly that I get goose bumps every time I think of them.

Soon after we had our second son, I had an astounding revelation: I had reached the light at the end of my long, sorrowful tunnel. As I stood in the brilliant glow peering back into the darkness of my past, I knew the worst was behind me.

It was odd to finally find myself in the warmth of that sacred light, basking in my family's love, soaking up God's splendor. And in that miraculous moment of realization, I thought to myself, *"Surely goodness and love will follow me all the days of my life, and I will dwell in the house of the Lord forever." (Psalm 23:6)*

Epilogue

fter my sons were born, I finally found myself in the light of pure love and happiness. But while the darkness seems miles behind me now, I will *never* forget my past.

Although I refuse to let my past rule my present, I cannot erase the tragedy from my childhood. For so many years, I kept it locked away, hidden from view, to protect myself and my family from reliving it again. But now, with this book, I am fulfilling my purpose in life: To share my story with the world about what the Lord has done for me.

Revealing my story to the world is an extreme act of faith. I feel like I am doing the unimaginable, stepping completely outside of my comfort zone. Deep inside, I do not want to expose my family. I do not want people to look at me and think of this terrible tragedy. But I also feel it is my duty to offer hope to others who have lived through similar horrific tragedies. It is my obligation to tell the world that with God, anything is possible. I owe that much to Him.

This realization about my purpose in life came to me during a fast. That night, with an empty stomach and an open heart, I was praying and asking God for a miracle. I have always wanted something supernatural to happen to me. I have always asked God to let me hear His voice or see angels like my Aunt Tatyana did on her death bed.

That night as I prayed, I suddenly began to remember my past. The details of my childhood, the tragedy and my painful struggle, appeared before me as clear as day as if I were watching a slideshow of my life. And that's when it dawned on me: Not only had I seen miracles in my life—I *was* a miracle! I did not need to hear a voice or see angels to know it was time. It was time to share my story with the world.

Then, the next morning, God granted my wish. Around five a.m., I woke suddenly to the sound of a voice. The voice spoke to me, clear as a bell. It said, *"Just have faith."*

At first, I thought my husband had forgotten to turn off a sermon we were listening to the night before. I woke up Paul and asked him. "No, I turned it off last night," he answered sleepily. "Go back to sleep."

But I could no longer sleep. I suddenly knew exactly what I had heard: It was God's voice. I was so full of joy and gratitude to God that He had answered my prayer. After hearing his voice, my mission in life became absolutely clear. That morning, I called all of my friends to share this miracle with them. I told them I had decided to share my life story, my testimony, with as many people as possible. I was going to start writing a book about how I overcame my family's tragedy through God's love.

Don't get me wrong: I do not believe I am some mystical person who has a special ability to prevail over tragedy. I do not live in a heavenly bubble where I feel no pain. I am still human. I will *always* experience fear and doubt and pain. Just like anyone else, I get angry, upset, frustrated— but I have learned to recognize these feelings immediately, put a stop to them and pray. I try to remember that God is watching me at all times. He knows my heart's desires, my motives.

Yes, I have overcome many obstacles in life, but my power comes from the Bible. Every day, I make the decision to follow Christ and conquer my fleshly desires. It was a painful process in the beginning, but it has led to awesome results. It has brought me a life abundant with peace, joy, hope and love. And I hope that my story will inspire others to allow Jesus into their hearts.

After my tragic childhood, I could easily have turned to drugs and destroyed my life. Fortunately, I did not take that path. As a matter of fact, I have never even taken a single drug, not even an anti-depressant. I have never seen a psychologist or psychiatrist. I have always simply trusted God to do His will. I am not perfect—not even close—but I try to do my best, and He knows the intentions and sincerity of my heart.

During my long, painful journey, God placed some special people in my path to help guide me and support me. First of all, he blessed me with my dear grandparents who tried their best to help me through my tragic childhood. He also brought my dear friend Julia into my life, Mrs. Miller and most importantly, my incredible husband Paul. But there were other people as well, and I would like to recognize some of them here.

My Papa's sister Ludmila has always been especially kind to me. When Julia got married, I had to move out of her family's apartment. My Aunt Ludmila opened her home to me. Although she had four children in a three-bedroom apartment, she graciously offered me one of the bedrooms. I could not believe she was willing to give me one of her rooms. On my wedding day, she looked deep into my eyes and cried tears of joy. She was like a mother to me. To this day, I am eternally grateful to her for her kind heart, and I always pray for her good health and happiness.

God also blessed my life with Emmanuel, another dear friend of mine from our youth group. She went to school with Julia and me, and she was my other best friend. Emmanuel was petite and very pretty, but she was feisty and tough— she had a strong personality. She always stood up for me in school. I spent many nights at her house, and her family fed me and always made me feel welcome. I still thank God for Emmanuel and her family.

Also, my mother's sister, Inna, was always incredibly kind to me. She would always give me money and little gifts. Aunt Inna did the best she could to make me feel loved and cared for, and I will never forget her kindness.

There were not many family members or friends who tried to encourage me or help me overcome my dreadful childhood, but there were some. While I cannot acknowledge each of them in this book, I want these precious people to know I will never forget their thoughtfulness. You know who you are...and I thank God for you.

Of course, I realize that everyone is preoccupied with their own problems, so I do not blame anyone for overlooking my childhood struggles. I have no hard feelings for any of my family members. But today, I remember how lost and alone I often felt as a child...I was desperate for guidance and support from the people around me. That's why I try to recognize this kind of sorrow in others and encourage those who are suffering. I believe that is what God calls on us to do, to carry each other's burdens. I always choose to look at Christ's example and try not to stumble on other people's poor choices.

When I reflect on my difficult childhood, I still have many unanswered questions. I may never fully understand why my mother and father made the choices they made. But God knows everything. He sees the deep intentions of our heart. Only He has all of the answers—and I plan to ask Him one day.

My heart aches when I think about the dear sisters and brother I lost. I miss them terribly. I still cannot comprehend how my mother could have committed such a horrific act, and I do not understand why these terrible things happened to my family…but there are no answers. However, I believe I will see them one day in the city of gold. When King David, in the Bible, lost his son he said, *"Can I bring him back again? I will go to him, but he will not return to me."* (2 Samuel 12:23) This thought floods my heart with peace and hope.

My family still does not fully understand why my mother did what she did. But most likely, she suffered from post-partum depression and her head injury ultimately led to her atrocious actions. However, we know for a fact that she was not herself for quite a while before the tragedy. She cried out for help, but no one could fully understand her condition at that time. Everyone had good intentions, but they all failed to truly understand her. The simple truth is there is no closure to my mother's actions, and I have learned to live with that. I do not know what kind of relationship my mother had with God. I will never know.

Today, we all have painful regrets about our past. My father, my mother's family, all of us—we all wish we could go back in time and do things differently. Of course, it is too late for that now. I just hope that by sharing my story, people will learn a lesson from my family's tragedy. I pray that not one child will ever have to suffer through what I endured. I believe we can learn a lot from our tragedies and prevent these terrible things from happening to others.

As I look back on my troubled past, I feel no hatred for Papa. I have forgiven him. After all, that is what Jesus commanded us to do. In the Lord's Prayer we pray, *"Forgive us our debts, as we also have forgiven our debtors." (Matthew 6:12)*

My father has apologized to me for the choices he made, and I have offered him my forgiveness. We are at peace. When I told him I was ready to reveal my story to the world, he said, "Darling, maybe if I did take care of you and gave you all I could, you would not be who you are today. God was your faithful father that I could not be."

At first, it pained me to hear him say those words. But then I realized what he said is true. It is written in the Bible

that God is "a father to the fatherless, a defender of widows."
(Psalm 68:5) His words strengthened my sense of purpose
in life, and they helped me make sense of my difficult childhood. "Yes Papa, you are right," I answered. "That is why
I'm writing this book...because I owe it to God."

Once I found God, I knew I did not want my family to live
a double life. I promised myself that my own family would
have a true relationship with God and a firm foundation.
And that is exactly what our family strives for every day.
We choose God to be the center of our life—and we are
so much stronger for it. In troubled times, when the storms
come, we stand strong together. And it's because God's
love dwells in our home.

I strive to be the best mother I can possibly be. I am
extremely careful never to use words that would put fear
into my children's lives. When I was a little girl, my mother
said my bad behavior would send her to an early grave.
Unfortunately, those words planted seeds of guilt and fear
in my heart at such young age. Of course, no matter what,
I loved my mother dearly. But today, I know the things she
told me were not right. I would never speak to my children
that way.

I take parenting extremely seriously, and I fully understand that my decisions are not just mine—all of the decisions I make today will directly affect my sons' lives, my

husband's life and of course my life. My children are proud to have me as their mom. They constantly tell me they wish I could stop working all the time and stay home with them. That request is on my prayer list.

I just look at my children and realize they are truly miracles from God. If I allowed my past to rule my present, I know that my sons would not be who they are today. Both of my children excel in school, and they are very happy. I believe my sons will live joyful, godly lives just as I try to do.

My husband and I also pray every day that we will always have a strong marriage. He tries to be the best husband he can be by obeying God's Word, and I pray every day that I can be like the wise woman who is described in the Proverbs 14:1: *"The wise woman builds her house, but with her own hands the foolish one tears hers down."*

I am so thankful to God for my husband. Paul has never doubted me. He always strives to be a man of God, and he loves to spend time with me and our boys.

Paul is still a talented singer, and he praises God with his beautiful voice. He sang to me at our wedding, and now he sings at almost every wedding we attend. He likes to dedicate the songs to me in front of everyone. I always feel a little guilty that all the attention turns to me and away from the bride and the groom. But deep inside, I wish for every husband and wife to be blessed like Paul and me—

always singing to each other and completely in love with one another.

God has used Paul in my life to make me a better person. He is my best friend, and I'm so proud to call him my husband. I love him dearly. Paul and I understand that we must put God first and family second. Everything else falls into place after those two. That is the secret to our joyful and fulfilling life, and I feel so blessed.

Throughout my journey, I have also learned how to protect my soul. To this day, I am very careful about what I listen to, read and watch. The Bible says our eyes are the doors to our heart: *"The eye is the lamp of the body. If your eyes are good, your whole body will be full of light. But if your eyes are bad, your whole body will be full of darkness. If then the light within you is darkness, how great is that darkness!" (Matthew 6:22)* That's why I try to filter out the evil and protect my mind, soul and spirit from anything that is not Godly. This works for me, and I wish for my children to do the same. We have to defend ourselves. I like to listen to music, watch movies and read books that build me up and make me feel stronger. I also strive to protect my health and my body. The Bible says my body is a temple of the Holy Spirit, so I want to keep it strong. I like to work out and stay as fit as possible. I want to be beautiful from the inside out—that is very important to me.

Everything I am today and everything I have, I owe to God. When I was trapped in the darkest depths of my past, God protected me. That is why I'm writing this book. I want to share my testimony with anyone who will listen. I want to encourage people. I want everyone to know that Jesus has the power to heal and restore your heart—even if your heart has been shattered into a million pieces by past tragedies. He will mend it, put the pieces back together and fill it with pure love.

We can be so religious all of our lives and still not have a true relationship with Jesus Christ. Even if we follow a set of rules and rituals, if we lack personal faith in God, we are simply wasting our time and efforts.

Today, I understand that God's joy is different from human happiness. Human happiness is directly affected by circumstances in life—but God's joy is so much stronger. When God entered my heart, I experienced pure, unadulterated joy for the first time in my life. And no matter what was happening in my life, if I always had Jesus in my heart, I would never lose my faith, hope and love.

My story is about surrendering all, having faith in God and honoring Him. Regardless of my tragic past, my painful childhood or my life's circumstances, I will always say, "Blessed be the name of the Lord."

Every day, I give thanks to God for guiding me through this journey. I have been delivered from unimaginable fear and pain, and I have discovered freedom through His love. I call on Jesus each and every day to help me and keep me under His protection and guidance. In the Bible, He promised, *"And surely I am with you always, to the very end of the age." (Matthew 28:20)* And I know this is true.

I have forgiven everyone. I have forgiven my mother. I have forgiven my father. I love him, and I wish only God's blessings to him. I live in peace, and I try to live to the fullest each and every day. I do my best, and I trust in God. I am truly blessed with two beautiful sons and a wonderful husband. Paul and I have faced mountains, but we know how to rise above them.

The secret to my victorious life is the Word of God. Read it, follow it, do what it says—and most importantly, *believe* it.

I survived a horrible tragedy and suffered through an anguished childhood. But I chose not to let my painful past tear away at my soul. Instead, God's unfailing love turned my tragedy into a pearl of hope. And now, I share this pearl with the world.

"But those who hope in the Lord will renew their strength. They will soar on wings like eagles; they will run and not grow weary, they will walk and not be faint." (Isaiah 40:31)

A Special Note for My Siblings

I write this in remembrance of Natasha, Misha, Vera, Alonna and baby Julia: I will never forget you, I will always love you and I will see you again in the golden city.

About the Author

Tatyana Alekseyevna is a happily married mother of two children, who currently resides in Georgia. *A Pearl of Hope* is her first book. Tatyana is available for Christian speaking events to share her story and offer hope and inspiration to those who are suffering. For more information, contact her at apearlofhope.com

CPSIA information can be obtained at www.ICGtesting.com
Printed in the USA
LVOW042354250912

300309LV00001B/2/P